Druidry and
the Ancestors

Druidry and the Ancestors

Nimue Brown

MOON
BOOKS

Winchester, UK
Washington, USA

First published by Moon Books, 2012
Moon Books is an imprint of John Hunt Publishing Ltd., Laurel House, Station Approach,
Alresford, Hants, SO24 9JH, UK
office1@jhpbooks.net
www.johnhuntpublishing.com
www.moon-books.net

For distributor details and how to order please visit the 'Ordering' section on our website.

Text copyright: Nimue Brown 2012

ISBN: 978 1 78099 677 6

A CIP catalogue record for this book is available from the British Library.

Design: Stuart Davies
Cover art: Tom Brown 2012

Printed and bound by CPI Group (UK) Ltd, Croydon, CR0 4YY

We operate a distinctive and ethical publishing philosophy in all
areas of our business, from our global network of authors to
production and worldwide distribution.

CONTENTS

Acknowledgements

Thank you Ronald Hutton, whose book *Blood and Mistletoe* did so much to crystallize my thoughts around the issues of ancient and revivalist Druidry, and who kindly cast an eye over the 'Spotting the melons' chapter.

My thanks to those other many authors whose words I have borrowed and whose history stories I have devoured. Their inspiration and vision has very much fed my own.

I must sweep a bow to Gary Cousins, who broadened my understanding of what ancestry means and without whose inspiring ideas I would never have taken on the subject.

My huge appreciation to Trevor Greenfield at Moon Books, who took on Druidry and Meditation with the clearly stated belief that he would be seeing more books from me. That went a long way towards giving me the courage to write this one.

Profound gratitude to my wonderful husband Tom Brown, who has walked with me through all the writing, researching, pondering and soul searching that the project involved. His love and compassionate wisdom have held me together for years now.

Thank you everyone who has read early versions, answered questions about research issues, loaned or given me books, pointed me at books and articles... especially my brother, Autumn Barlow, Cat Treadwell, and the good folk at www.honour.org.uk. Also thanks to those who generously shared stories but who did not wish to be named. You have made this possible. Any mistakes and confusion in the mix should be attributed to me, however.

I'd also like to thank the band of intrepid souls who read and comment on my blog at www.Druidlife.wordpress.com I use the blog to work through ideas and see how people respond to them, and have learned a lot from my commentators. The ongoing challenges to refine my thinking have done me a great deal of good as a writer, and as a person.

Finally, I give thanks to my ancestors.

Introduction

In some ways it is easier to explain what this book isn't, than to begin by pinning down what it is.

This is not a history book in the sense of having lots of dates and hard, dependable information about the history of Druidry in it. It definitely isn't a linear narrative history of Druidry at all. It is, however, a book about history, with the emphasis on the *story*. This is an exploration of how we imagine and construct our ancestors, and what the implications are of the ways in which we think about them. Anyone interested in the history of Druidry, I would suggest reads both Ronald Hutton's *Blood and Mistletoe* and Graeme K Talboys' *The Way of the Druid*, which are highly informative and offer very different understandings of the subject. It's not the facts of history I want to explore, but what we do with them.

This is also not a book designed to teach a person how to do Druidry. It is, I hope, something that would be of use to anyone exploring a Druid path, to people in the wider pagan community, and to anyone with an interest in the ancestors. We all have ancestors and, for most of us, that can be a complicated issue. This is a book about making peace with the ancestors, understanding their legacies and their ongoing presence in our lives, and exploring how ancestry impacts on community, and ideas of race, nation and culture. For someone looking for a book that will help them begin the study of Druidry, I recommend Graeme K Talboys' *The Druid Way Made Easy* and Robin Herne's *Old Gods, New Druids*.

One of the things I do want to do is raise the issue of how we access history. Many pagan readers and authors alike are self-taught people. Working outside formal academia, dependant on what we can find and not always aware of where the cutting edge is, we are a community vulnerable to misinformation and

I

being horribly out of date. Mistakes made by authors fifty or a hundred years ago still surface in pagan writing and new examples of that surface all the time. I recently read a book that claimed 'The Hallstatt Celts (named for a region of Austria where their culture originated) were the earliest Celtic group to reach Caledonia.'[1] Hallstatt Celts didn't originate there; it was simply the location of some finds that went on to define our understanding of that period. How many readers will go on to transmit the error as fact? Did the author acquire it in all innocence, or through lack of due care and attention? The same book offers it as a certainty that the 'Coligny calendar' constitutes evidence of Druid astronomical understanding. It doesn't even mention the issues of interpretation and uncertainty around this fascinating item. The Coligny calendar finds its way into a lot of commentary on the Druids and Celts, along with the idea of Pythagoras being taught by Druids, and a great many other unsubstantiated or over interpreted details. As pagan readers we're still afflicted by the influence of figures like Gimbutas and Margaret Murray, the wild imaginings of antiquarians, and a plethora of other dubious sources. Picking threads of truth from this messy heap is not easy.

A poor understanding of our own history does not allow us to deal well with history as presented in the mainstream. It encourages an inaccurate understanding of who we are as a religious people and where we came from. We can easily get snarled up by other people's 'facts' – The British Museum thinks Lindow Man was a victim of Druid ritual murder. Ronald Hutton disputes this. It pays us, as a community, to be skeptical about history, and historians, especially when there is so clearly no one agreed upon 'truth'. It is important to be able to differentiate between an indisputable fact and a speculation. Most historical writing involves some degree of guesswork. We need to differentiate between what can be inferred, reasonably, from a piece of evidence, and what is plain assumption. Sometimes writers offer inferences as the only possible way of making sense of something, when that's seldom the case. When guesses are presented in a language of authority, it is hard to tell which bits are certain, and where gaps have been filled with imagination. Hutton is my personal hero in this regard, with his willingness to express the limitations of fact and to make sure all speculation is clearly stated as such. His writing has sensitized me to the lack of such clarity in other histories.

Working with other people's mistakes, we as pagans can also very easily make ourselves look like fools, as with the Hallstatt example above. If we're working with theories that are a hundred years out of date, or based on something widely known to be a forgery, we are open to criticism, and rightly so.

Part of the problem here is the tension between spiritual truth as known by an individual, and the kind of truth that is recognized by the rest of the world. There are plenty of goddess worshippers who know that Gimbutas was right about ancient matrilineal societies, that the feminist pagan movement inspired by her was right, and know that nine million women in Europe were burned at the stake for witchcraft. There are plenty of Druids who know that Druid organizations and wisdom have survived intact since ancient times. There are also people who 'know' that the holocaust didn't happen, so this is not a simple issue. There are many stories out there, and many people who consider them true, regardless of the available evidence.

My purpose is not to denigrate anyone's personal truth, but to help fellow pagans hold a dual perception of the world. I am increasingly convinced that we need to be able to think about all things in two ways, and to hold those simultaneously. We need to be able to recognize and work with the fruits of rationality as they manifest both in academic work and in the mainstream. We also need our more private knowings, and critically, we have to know which is which. We need to be able to think analytically about 'truth' as it is handed to us by others – no matter who they are, and to think in just the same way about the truths we construct for ourselves.

In modern Druid ritual, we normally honor our ancestors. This is usually a brief business, undertaken after either the four quarters or the three worlds have been hailed. A typical honoring in ritual would go something like this: 'Hail blessed ancestors, you of our blood, you whose bones are in this soil and whose wisdom guides us. We thank you for your blessings as we gather for this ritual today. ' Then, at the end of the ritual as things unwind, a few words of thanks might also be offered.

Sometimes Samhain rituals bring a deeper focus on our ancestors, but for the greater part of the time, this is the current level of conscious attention they enjoy in contemporary Druid ritual. Part of the point of this book is to argue that those few lines are not enough, and to demand that we do more. We need to understand ourselves within in the context of our actual ancestry, and the ancestries we, and others, have imagined. I want to explore how our understanding of the past, and explicitly our ancestors, informs who we are and where we might be going. I also want to look at how we use and reimagine the past for our own purposes.

Modern Druidry exists with a historical context that is both complex and frequently challenging. The material we draw upon is not exclusively ancient, and the means by which it has come to us is not always the most honorable. I think these are issues we need to face head on as we construct ourselves and our religion. In this aspect, I am hugely indebted to Ronald Hutton's Blood and Mistletoe.

Some years before I even considered writing this book, I arranged for a workshop on ancestry, led by Gary Cousins. I organized the technical bits, including chasing round to encourage attendance. I ran repeatedly into the same reaction – folk who felt so uncomfortable about their immediate ancestry that the idea of any serious work in that area alarmed them. Most modern pagans come from non-pagan backgrounds, and for many that can be a source of tension and discomfort. It can act as a barrier between ourselves and the past. Part of the aim of this book therefore is to explore how we make peace with our own ancestry.

This last year has sent me on an unexpected journey into my own ancestry, so I'll be drawing on that too. Tales from actual life are often more resonant than theoretical ideas.

These are the various ideas that have motivated me in putting this book together. While I am writing from a Druid perspective, I am confident that many of the issues are to some degree relevant for anyone on a pagan path, and hopefully beyond. We all have ancestors, they are part of our shared humanity and while historically ancestry, especially in the guise of race, has been used as a tool to divide, it is also a commonality that might yet help us move in greater harmony.

Chapter One

Defining the Ancestors

The current interest in Druidism depends not so much upon the ancient past as upon very recent history.[2]

The three Druidic ancestors

Modern Druidry identifies three groups of ancestors. They are the ancestors of blood, the ancestors of place, and the ancestors of tradition. There is plenty of scope for overlap between the three, but in separating them out, we have scope to think creatively and to make deliberate choices about how we identify ourselves with them. The choosing and constructing of ancestors is, I think, an activity most pagans engage in to some degree, although how conscious the process is, I am less certain. I imagine we all have different levels of consciousness about the stories we construct.

Frequently, ancestor construction is a shared project, and one that moves forward all the time. Envisaging the ancestors is often far more about trying to figure out who we are than anything really to do with them. While that self-understanding agenda is important, holding a wider, more honest and perhaps more accurate picture would be advantageous. Later on I will be exploring in depth how each of the three ancestral groups function and how we might relate to them. First it makes sense to consider the full breadth that ancestry implies.

It is most usual to consider ancestors purely as being those of blood. However, the inclusion of ancestors of place and tradition open us to much wider ways of contemplating our ancestral heritage and may be less familiar to people who are not already on the Druid path. It also draws into the mix an element of choice. Our blood lines may be beyond our control, but in choosing where we live and work, we choose our ancestors of place. Our traditions are entirely a matter of choice, as are the ancestors were thereby select for ourselves, allowing us total freedom to place ourselves in any context or conceptual lineage we find appealing. This would not always have been an option for our blood ancestors. For someone whose blood ancestry is unknown, or is a source of grief or insufficiency, this option to choose is incredibly liberating.

When we think about ancestors, it is important to remember that we too will be ancestors of the future. Again this shift away from the simple ancestry of blood is important. There is more to continuation than the passing down of your genetic material. A person who is unable or who chooses not to breed will still be an ancestor of place to future generations. That impact is unavoidable and important. However, it is only through the legacy we leave in our work that we might become future ancestors of tradition. We cannot entirely choose this role for ourselves and will never see what the true extent of our impact is.

There is no single, coherent narrative approach for how modern, western pagans should relate to their ancestors. Looking around the world at the practices of indigenous and traditional peoples, we can find all kinds of models for how we might exist in relationship with our ancestors. However, any practice we consider in this way belongs to a people, a tribe, a culture and a history that are not directly our own. It is of course a different matter if they are ours, and tapping into traditions you do belong to can provide a simple solution to all this. However, for the white westerner, there are no tribal myths or ancient rituals of ancestor honoring. We will have to develop our own.

I have no doubt that we can productively learn by considering what other cultures do. The wholesale borrowing of other people's beliefs and ways of living is not always honorable though, nor is it reliably helpful. Relationship with the ancestors is not a concept that can ever exist in isolation. It belongs to place and time, to ways of life, to art, story and life experience. The ancestors are not separate from life as we live it, but intrinsic to it. We need to see them as part of our community, not a few extra lines in a ritual. A modern, western pagan with no ancestral tradition of reverencing the ancestors cannot simple take someone else's approach and assume it will work out of context.

All that remains to us, therefore, is the tricky process of building new traditions. Modern paganism has been doing just this for a good fifty years now. It is the essence of moots, intrinsic to every new branch of paganism that flourishes, vital for any aspiring teacher. We are in the collective process of making a new story and constructing new ways of being. How long they will serve we cannot know. Many practices do not outlive their originator. Some are discarded a few years after being thought up. Others turn out to be durable enough, and resonant enough, to be shared and passed on. Perhaps these will survive for years, or even generations. We have no way of knowing.

What humans want from tradition is a way of doing things that creates a feeling of connection and involvement. Whether we want to feel part of the cycle of the seasons, part of the land, or the chain of ancestry, it is the involvement that matters most. Tradition gives a form to the involvement that has the additional prestige of being old. Being passed down through time lends weight and credibility to the strangest and least comprehensible of practices. Traditions tend to evolve and change over time, as susceptible to innovation and external pressures as anything else. Somehow even if they have evolved beyond all recognition from the original, the idea that we are part of a tradition still gives that all-important sense of connection. Most of us want to belong, somewhere.

The ancestors of modern paganism are very recent. Some have passed over, many still live. Their names are still known to us.

Whether we seek to venerate them, or race to throw out their ideas and replace them with our own, will vary. Whether in a few hundred years time anyone remembers them as ancestors, remains to be seen. How we construct our understanding of ancestry is not just about these high profile figures in our traditions, however. It's about how we view ourselves and our blood lines and story lines, about what we want to pass down, and how we undertake to make sense of the world and our place within it.

The ancestors of Druidry

We have a vague collective awareness of ancient Druids, as a religious group associated with Celtic peoples. As Ronald Hutton went to some length to demonstrate in Blood and Mistletoe, all of the written information about the Druids has come from other sources, and none are without issue. In a much older text, archaeologist Stuart Piggott also explained there are no sites featuring a word for 'Druid' that give us a definite link between physical evidence and Druidry.[3] Outside those uncertain classical texts, we can only infer Druidic practice by first assuming the presence of Druids. Consequently, there are many things we 'know' that could be true, but no indisputable facts. However, the past few hundred years have been full of speculation about the early Druids, including all kinds of ideas that probably had no historical accuracy. Picking through these is very difficult, not least because the ideas and images are so widespread, like the claims for a Stonehenge association, human sacrifice and the white-nighty-robes. None of this necessarily has anything much to do with our ancient Druid ancestors.

In his books, Graham Talboys makes a case for the survival of bardic schools and the transmission of Druidry by other means. If 'Druid' basically meant the educated classes, then Druidic ideas will have survived in stories, wisdom teachings, and so forth. It's a very tempting argument, and one my heart wants to believe even if my head remains uncertain. I hold a duel understanding of this theory. I feel it as truth; I accept it intellectually as unproven. This is entirely comfortable for me.

If our ancient Druid ancestors were complicated, the more recent ones are far more troublesome. The Druid revival began with antiquarians. Archaeology was a new science, for which the rule books had yet to be written. Men with all kind of drums to bang and personal theories to shoehorn in somewhere piled in. Men with political agendas looking for icons to work with. Men who just wanted some fame and money and weren't too fussy how they got there. Yet from amongst the flights of fancy, forgeries and self importance of the Druid revival, came the seeds that have grown into modern Druidry. Just as we may look back at our blood ancestry with mixed feelings, so too can we find our ancestors of tradition are a challenging lot as well.

Understanding that influence, and facing up to it, is essential. We need to own the story, warts and all. Some of the prayers we use in modern ritual, the forms themselves, and even the cherished awen symbol probably originated with Iolo Morganwg, a man set on forgery and self aggrandizement, who used those around him and betrayed every Druid principle he ever put on paper. His inspiration was beautiful, his life was not. We can make our peace with that.

Mark Lindsey Earley, writing in the handbook for Exeter's Bardic Chair sums the situation up in this way:

It is worth pointing out, at this juncture, that the historical accuracy of Iolo's claims is highly dubious and that in all likelihood no such 'ancient manuscripts' ever existed, despite his ironic espousal of the bardic/Druidic motto 'The truth against the World'! However, we think it's rather harsh to label such an important 'hero' of the movement as an out-and-out fraud. A more mystical perspective might theorise that he 'channeled' his information. At the very least we like to think that he was creatively inspired, and that, although the history he outlined was possibly a purely 'romantic' one, it is no less important or valid, as long as we distinguish it from academic history.[4]

The less we make outlandish claims about our historical heritage, the better. The more we focus on our behavior in this time, the better. We need to know how we got here and how that shapes us, and we need to hold a realistic understanding of what modern Druidry is, and where it comes from. With that in place, we have room to talk quietly about the other ways of knowing, the heartfelt truth, the wisdom inherent in trees and the land that comes down to us regardless of human foibles, or any other story that we feel compelled to share. Stories are wondrous things, but it's important not to confuse them with anything else.

Robert Graves

I want to take a brief detour through an example now and talk about a specific ancestor. He's an ancestor of tradition for me, but he's also a figure caught up in the complexities of academic history-making, the emerging Druid tradition and his own blood lines. He is a character who represents much of what this book is about.

My dad bought The White Goddess when I was fairly small, and talked about it. I think I absorbed the idea of a triple goddess round about then, such that it took me years to realize that it wasn't an absolute fact of ancient belief. I have no idea what else entered my young mind as a certainty. So I came to Robert Graves through my own blood ancestry. I studied his poetry in detail whilst doing A-level English literature, and went on to read The White Goddess myself during my college years. By then I'd read a little Frazer, and had just enough contact with things academic to realize I was reading poetry, not history. Later on again, I started to see where others had taken Graves as history and quoted it. His tree calendar, in particular, comes up as 'fact' in places that don't mention him specifically, or any other sources.

While I was working on this book, an essay on Graves came to me purely by chance, thanks to an OBOD egroup. On closer inspection it turned out that the author, Peter Berresford Ellis, is an English historian, literary biographer and novelist who has published over 90 books and has an MA in Celtic studies, according to that great fount of all wisdom; Wikipedia. It makes him more the expert than Graves.

Peter Berresford Ellis, in his essay The Fabrication of 'Celtic' Astrology[5] talks about the misleading influence of Graves, whose work on the tree calendar has become so pervasive. He points out: 'Robert Graves relied on 19th Century translations, and often very bad translations as well as texts that were quite counterfeit. Indeed, texts which were simply mere inventions. He was inclined to late 18th and 19th Century Welsh romantics ('gentlemen antiquarians') rather than reliable scholars.' This ties in with the points I want to make about ongoing confusion and dodgy scholarship, where other pagan authors are still drawing, sometimes indirectly, on all the same sources (Iolo Morganwg for example). We know there has been forgery and fantasy; what the vast majority of pagan readers do not know, myself included, is just how far spread those misleading influences are.

Graves went on to compound his mistakes by not listening to the advice of others who had worked in greater length and depth studying his field. I could argue that he rejected the knowledge of his immediate ancestors of tradition. Apparently it goes further. Graves had a poor relationship with his own father and, as a consequence, seems to have missed the resources of his paternal grandfather, who was, 'both Professor of Mathematics at TCD, and a leading authority on Ogham. He was an expert on the ancient law system of Ireland, the Brehon Law, and convinced the London Government to establish a Royal Commission to rescue, edit and translate the surviving texts, which was done through 1865-1901.'[6] Furthermore…

In 1876, Dr Charles Graves contributed a paper to the academic journal Hermathena (published by Trinity College, Dublin) on 'The Ogam Alphabet'. For the first time, he pointed out that surviving Ogham inscriptions had been written at the beginning of the Christian period and 'the extreme pagan theory could no longer be maintained'. He examined the claims made about Ogham in the Auraicept and the allied tracts on Ogham (not noted by O'Flaherty) such as Duil Feda ind Ogaim (Book of Ogham Letters) and a second text Duil Feda na Forfid (Book of Extra Letters). These texts did appear in George Calder's edition of Auraicept na nÉces (Edinburgh, 1917), which Robert had supposedly read and quoted from.

Peter Berresford Ellis concludes that had Robert Graves been able to consult with Dr Charles Graves he might have been able to write a more accurate and useful book than The White Goddess. One can only imagine what has been lost to modern paganism as a consequence.

This is a story of the ancestry of modern paganism. It is also a story of a man at odds with his blood family, trying to prove himself in a field he is not well qualified in. It is an obvious illustration of what happens when mistakes are compounded, one upon another, through lack of awareness of the past. Here is an example not to follow.

Ronald Hutton also comments on the relationship between Graves and previous, suspect work, including mistranslated Welsh material, the fabrications of Iolo Morganwg, and the work of James Frazer, concluding that Graves 'built a fantasy upon a forgery.'[7]

And yet... I remember how I felt on reading The White Goddess. For the first time in my young life, I had a sense of real mystery and magic. I felt that something amazing was there, just beyond my capacity to grasp it. I wondered if, with years of study and rigor I might one day be able to come back and penetrate the dense tangle of briars and understand what the roebuck is all about. I felt the book keenly even as I struggled with it intellectually. It marked me, creating for me an idea of achieving insight and forging a whole new relationship with reality. It might be fair to say that I've been trying to grasp that mystery ever since. I know I am not alone in this.

Graves as an ancestor of tradition for me is no less powerful for having been arrogant, misguided and oblivious to the work of his blood ancestor. The hunger for something profound and numinous, is real, no matter who awakens it or how sullied their own methods may be. The heritage of inspiration is there to be claimed and kept no matter what the factual history looks like. We can separate them out.

Who are the ancestors?

Most of us know who our immediate ancestors were, but the precise details soon peter out, leaving only a vague impression of those who lived as little as a few hundred years ago. Although genealogy is a popular hobby, for most of us, those people before our immediate ancestors are an uncertain, amorphous lot, colored by whatever we learned of history at school, who we imagine our people were, and the odd focal story – a famous predecessor, a family legend, some speculation based on names. I have a huge family tree, mapped out by my uncle and delving deep into the past. Names, dates, jobs and occasional details are in the mix. It's interesting, but beyond those tantalizing glimpses, it tells me relatively little about how they lived, felt and thought. There aren't many facts, and the facts are not that informative. Unless people leave detailed letters and diaries, this is often the way of it. The ancestors remain mysterious.

For many of us, ideas held about ancestry are intimately connected to ideas of race and culture. Those on the far right believe in ancestry as a contained, defined thing, linking certain groups of people whilst distancing them from others. This seems to me a rather short sighted view of the past. Humans have been mobile and interbreeding for a very long time. We are all humans. But even for people who do not hold overtly racist views, race is important, perhaps connecting them directly to the history of a country, an area of land or a religion. The trouble is that recorded history is actually sparse, and as a percentage of human history, represents a very small bit. The further back you go, the less there is by way of written record. The countries and religions we have are relatively recent innovations, but our most recent history is inevitably the most resonant, and the most divisive. For anyone wanting to uphold the idea of division and separateness, recent history must be treated as more important than the ambiguous millennia preceding it. For anyone wishing to work with ideas of commonality, it becomes necessary to push past recorded human history in search of a time when perhaps ideas of race and culture did not divide us. A past we can only really imagine and can never hope to prove.

Assuming my family have not been in the habit of marrying off cousins too often... I have four grandparents, and eight great grandparents. So that's sixteen ancestors in the generation before them, thirty two, sixty four, one hundred and twenty eight... heading back a mere seven generations – a few hundred years, I might have two hundred and fifty four direct ancestors. Although given what I know of my paternal grandfather's side, it's probably a smaller number. But it makes the point. Humans have been here for a very long time, such that the numbers of our ancestors are vast to the point of being unimaginable. All those individual lives occurred, without which we would not exist as we are. All those choices of mate, all those survivals against the odds, resulted in us. The sheer scale of what it has taken to get to the point of us, is both daunting and potential food for an expanding ego.

Our human ancestry takes us right back to the very beginning of humanity, whenever and wherever that was. We share more immediate, common human ancestors with so many of the people around us. In places where there hasn't been much movement of peoples, that shared ancestry can be pronounced – Iceland for example. Even today in rural communities, people can knowingly have complex blood ties to a lot of people in their village. However, thinking of 'the ancestors' as a single, homogenous group who can be related to on mass, is not, I think, always a good idea. Ancestry, be it personal or cultural, spans huge expanses of time, covers broad arrays of beliefs and values, many of which may be entirely at odds with our own. Inevitably I'm going to use 'ancestors' loosely at times to mean innumerable and unnamed people, because if I caveat every statement the book will become both very long and rather painful to read.

'The ancestors' are all individuals. They belong to their own times, places, distinct social groupings, and eras. Even as we generalize, it is vital to hang on to that sense of them as all being separate, unique people. We might of course opt to believe that once departed, our ancestors blend their essences into a great communal ancestral melting pot of spirit, creating a resource that can indeed be called 'the ancestors' and which embodies all of them, merged together into one seamless thing. In some ways this idea is very convenient, which is partly why I dislike it. A universal, ancestral mush requires little thought from us, we can just draw upon them and seek their help when we feel like it, although what we would get back from that, I am uncertain. The idea negates individual humanity for those involved, and enables us to turn our ancestry into something simple and comfortable. That our actual ancestry is invariably complicated and challenging, matters in terms of how we understand and construct ourselves.

It might be literally true that we all share a common ancestry. If you imagine the first stirrings of life, back in the primordial stew at the dawn of time, and think that we all descended from there, then ancestry connects us to all other living things. We certainly have ancestry that isn't recognizably human, the mammals having evolved from something else in the first place. When fetuses develop, we go through the forms of the past. Our ancestry is acted out in each of our bodies as they form. We share so much genetic material with our fellow mammals that it is tempting to think of them as cousins, and to view our ancestral heritage as a shared one. If we are thinking in terms of ancestors of place, then it is very easy to include the vast non-human ancestry around us. This too has shaped the land and contributed to what we experience. From trees who are now coal, to the dead who make up the fertility in the soil, non-human ancestors have a huge impact on our daily lives; one that can be easily overlooked.

There is a choice to make here. We can decide to be entirely human-centric in our notions of ancestry, or we can embrace the wider possibility that we have common ancestry with all life on this planet. This has considerable implications for how we see ourselves, our place in the scheme of things, and how we relate to all other living beings. As a species, our self-image has been one of superiority, and for much of the last two thousand years in Europe we have understood ourselves as separate from the rest of nature, and 'special'. We told ourselves that we were made in god's image and that nature existed to serve us. The state of our planet cries out for a more realistic story about our place here, and our status.

If we reject this human-centric version of our history and instead embrace a wider ancestry, we place ourselves within nature. We acknowledge all that exists as being part of our family and in so doing we are obliged to understand ourselves differently as well.

I was first introduced to the idea of ancestry connecting us to all things by Gary Cousins, to whom I owe a significant debt. As I understand it, his shamanic paganism gives him a world view in which all experiences can be understood in terms of ancestry.

There is no reincarnation, only that which is played out in our bloodlines. This is not my own interpretation of existence, but has been a significant influence on my own developing thinking. Gary taught me that when we contemplate the enormity of ancestry, we can see there is little new. Whatever life brings to us, has been experienced before – or something very much like it. All the wisdom in the world lies with the ancestors. All the experience, the solutions and all the roots of today's problems lie there too. The more we do to understand our ancestors, to hear them, and learn from them, the better able we are to live our own lives.

All of human history can be understood as being our ancestry in an entirely immediate and personal way. If we relate to history as happening to other people and focus on the otherness of their times, beliefs and cultures, it's easy to pay them scant attention. If we claim whatever is known of our history as a personal thing, as our inheritance, if we embrace it and work with it, we have much to gain.

History and ancestry are intimately linked, but neither comes to us as hard and certain fact. They are both kinds of story that we tell to ourselves. Story telling has been with humans for a long time. I like to think it goes back to the beginnings of language, to camp fires and winter nights. The stories we tell about the past are also the stories we are telling about ourselves, and understanding that process is part of the journey into working with our ancestors.

Alongside the Druidry work, I am a fiction writer. The impulse to create story is familiar to me. I've also studied psychology, and poked around as an enthusiastic amateur in scientific and historical writing. Stories, as I see it, are at the core of how we express our humanity. We tell each other stories to explain things, to make sense of the world and our place in it. One of the key ideas underpinning counseling is that by getting a person to tell their story, they gain control of it, and no longer feel overpowered by whatever trauma they have experienced. Stories are a form of medicine. Clarissa Pinkola Estes' book, Women Who Run With Wolves[8] is entirely about the power of stories to teach and heal. She explains that stories have the power to transform and that some story telling traditions are all about healing work. I believe there is a magic in the creation and sharing of story that has vast power to influence how we think and therefore live.

Stories about our ancestors can tell us something about where we fit. For a person whose immediate ancestry offers no sense of comfort, reaching into a known, or imagined past can create the sense of belonging we all need to feel. Sometimes this is a life enhancing process, but it also has the potential to be destructive, taking us into fantasy, or fanaticism, widening the gulf between us and those around us, or enabling us to uphold unrealistic beliefs about ourselves. It is important to look at how we place ourselves in the context of both our known, and our imagined ancestry.

We make myths. We tell the stories of our own lives. One of the most frequent tales to share in a social gathering will begin 'Do you remember when we...?' and in telling the tale of something shared, bonds of community are reinforced. Children love to hear stories of their own early lives, affirming their sense of self. Lovers recount tales of how they first came together and in old age, we tell the stories of our lives to our descendants so that they will remember us. Equally we know our own immediate ancestors not only from our experience of them, but also through the stories they tell about themselves.

Our relationship with the more distant ancestors is part of both personal and collective mythmaking. Like any myth, that has the potential to enchant and inspire, but equally our myths can inhibit and mislead us. Understanding the process of mythmaking, the nature of our relationship with our ancestors and the ways in which these things affect us, can contribute significantly to how we live our lives. There is a great deal the ancestors can teach us, and not only in a spiritual or esoteric sense.

Deeper relationship with the ancestors calls for scrutiny of all things, careful thinking, and greater self-awareness. It requires that we contemplate our own myths, and give more conscious thought to the future. We need our ancestors, for the insight they will give us, for the history that is uniquely ours, and for self-knowledge. We may decide to define ourselves in opposition to them, but if we pay them no attention, we run the very real risk of repeating their mistakes.

Finding and identifying ancestors

There are plenty of practical ways in which we can go about researching our ancestors – directly through family stories, following the genealogy route, exploring local history, and reinforcing this by reading more general historical information about how people used to live in different periods. Should we have any famous ancestors, more information may be available about their lives. We may equally find a letter writer or journal keeper whose words are then available to us, providing a direct link with the past. As I commented before, however, the quest for direct ancestors might furnish us with dates and a few details, but not necessarily much sense of who they were and how they lived.

It's often easy to see some of the legacy of our ancestors of place just by looking around, but again the journey from surface detail to insight is a tricky one. I'm writing this on a narrowboat. The waterway my boat floats on was built by hand, by navies – many of whom were Irish. The historical narrowboat people came to this way of life out of necessity – as I have done. Sharing the space and aware of the history, I feel a degree of connection with these ancestors of place. And yet I know nothing of any of them as individuals. My impressions are hazy and general. Even living so close to their way of life, I cannot know them rationally or individually.

Ancestors of tradition are often the easiest folk to identify. These are the people who shape, guide and teach us. I can point to the people I learned some of my Druidry from. I know their names, I can ask them questions. These ancestors are still alive and entirely available to me. Similar things can be said of my writing influences, the living folk musicians I've been inspired by and, to a fair extent, anyone named and historical who I consider an influence. These are my chosen ancestors and I have selected them as specific individuals. Most people could identify a comparable selection informing their own tradition. In taking inspiration from someone, we are likely to know who they are and thus able to form deeper relationship with them, by whatever means seem appropriate.

However, if your tradition is longer than one human lifespan, it will have its share of the nameless within it. Druidry is no exception. We know the names of some of the major figures in the development of modern Druidry, but when it comes to our ancient ancestors of tradition, we have very little to work with.

Finding the ancestors has the potential to be a huge labor of academic research, far beyond the capabilities of most of us. While we can look to historians and archaeologists for insight, we are limited by the things history simply cannot tell us about. Even the finding of a religious artifact from ancient history doesn't tell us how the people who made it felt, what they dreamed about or secretly prayed for. Often it seems to be those elusive details that we most need. What kinds of hats our ancestors wore is of very little emotional significance compared to their beliefs. The hats we might be able to learn about. No one will ever excavate a belief, and anything we find that might pertain to it, must be interpreted through the inhibiting filters of our own perceptions and understandings.

We come quickly to a point of difficulty. The ancestry we most need, in a spiritual and emotional sense, is the ancestry that is least available to us. The chances of there ever being clear, coherent and reliable evidence for how all of our spiritual ancestors felt about the world, understood it, or held their beliefs seems unlikely. One of the commonly held assertions is that the ancient Druids did not write anything down, which puts us at a distinct disadvantage. No one has yet found anything that has been defined as writing by ancient Druids about Druids. Finding such a thing would undermine the very stories we've been depending on, unhelpfully.

Does that automatically invalidate all questing after our ancestry? No. It leaves us with tools based on insight and experience, and on what is often described as 'unsubstantiated personal gnosis'. It leaves us with myth, imagination and some difficult waters to navigate.

Here it is important to flag up the difference between ancestry and history. History as a subject clearly depends on a study of everyone's ancestors, and often it is the sense of having some commonality that makes the past interesting to us. History as an academic subject has distinct rules about the sourcing and presentation of material. It is concerned not only with facts, but the ways in which we understand and interpret them. Modern history writers are alert to the possibility of multiple interpretations. History is itself an evolving subject with its own narrative. The ancestors of historical study were all people, existing in their own time and place, and inevitably colored by that. Thus history is a subject continually remaking itself.

Popular history, as represented in the media, is frequently rather different to academic history. It overlaps with drama and storytelling far more. Words may be put into the mouths of historical figures for dramatic effect. Subject matter tends to revolve around the sensational, not around the fine details of the degree to which a source is reliable. Pop history is far more about the story, and the exiting big names in it, than about hard fact. It can be misleading, at best. Edward Vallance observed in 2009, that history-based programs on television were 'focusing almost exclusively on the actions of kings and queens', and described the content as 'sexed-up'.[9] I don't think much has changed since then. This creates a bias in the ways many of us think about the past, as certain ideas, and types of people are kept invisible.

Ancestry is not an academic discipline, it is simply the totality of human and perhaps also non-human life prior to our own. Within that, it can represent as much or as little as we choose. Ancestry is only meaningful to us when it is in some way personal, or emotionally engaged with. Cultures that venerated and worshipped ancestors in the past may well have been looking for mediation between the living and the spirit realms. I think modern, western peoples may well be more interested in self-validation, feeling a sense of connection or seeking inspiration. Ancestry as a term has the potential to mean almost everything, which is vast to the point of being almost useless conceptually. The deliberate choosing and focusing brings a lot of the meaning to our experience of ancestry. Thus the ways in which we choose our ancestors and what we then undertake to do with them, has the scope to be of great significance to us. It is not necessarily a rational or even a deliberate process, however.

Finding our ancestors in a spiritual or emotional sense is inevitably very different from finding them in an evidenced sense. Like all quests, the journey will probably tell us more about ourselves than the intended quarry. This is in many ways an argument for taking up the exploration rather than rejecting it. As we search for meaning in our ancestry, it is vitally important to discriminate between what is definite fact, what is speculative, and what comes to us from more imaginative ways of knowing. I think all of these approaches are valid so long as we retain the ability to differentiate between them. An academic awareness of history is not the same as an experiential relationship with the ancestors based on living as they have done. Neither is 'better' and each has the potential to enhance the other. Both bring uncertainties and areas of doubt. We can fill the spaces of doubt with our imaginations. The problems begin when people make those imaginative gap-fillers and then believe they have uncovered 'truth'. The history of modern Druidry is littered with these difficult moments, as with the Robert Graves story, and it would be as well not to perpetuate them.

Chapter Two

History as Story

It is not possible to ever be truly objective when it comes to our understanding of human behavior. We exist in a cultural context, with a story about how the world works. The current story probably doesn't match the stories our ancestors had. I do not know to what degree it is possible to understand our own biases and the ways in which they influence our thoughts, much less anyone else's. Simply to recognize they might exist and could influence us would be a good place to start.

Philip Carr-Gomm observes an extra layer of difficulty for pagan readers, that there are:

> *Two ideologies – two ways of looking at life: the one materialist, the other spiritual. Our interpretation of history will depend upon which ideology or philosophy we favor, and until we grasp the way in which each stance affects the interpretation of the past, or study of Druids will be confusing in the extreme. Most books about the Druids have combined factual historical material with esoteric or speculative material in a way that is often unclear and which leads to accusations from academics that the authors have combined fantasy with fact.*[10]

The habit in all 'serious' writing for a long time was to present the narrator as neutral observer, and the facts as nice and solid. Many publications still demand this style. There is an increasing willingness in writers of non-fiction of all subjects to try to flag up what their own inherent biases might be so that readers can better understand what they are being told and assess it for themselves. Sat here with my rather lopsided writing hat on, it's all too easy to see the limitations of this approach as well. What do you need to know about me for the purposes of this book? My age and gender? I've indicated my being a pagan Druid already. I must admit to not being a trained historian, philosopher or anthropologist. On the academic side, I'm armed only with a degree in English literature and a moderate amount of reading around. Is that the measure of my intellectual worth as a commentator? I can only hope not. Perhaps we need to discuss my class background and how that impacts on my understanding of humanity, or my personal financial situation and how that might inform a desire to earn money from my writings. Would my bank balance make me inclined to be more, or less controversial? And what of my politics? (Green).

One thing I do know to be relevant is that I am English, I have always lived in England, and both my Druidry and my sense of the ancestors exists in the context of that Englishness. I am very conscious that both Druidry and ancestry will be very different issues for people in different countries. There is no way in which I can write from beyond my own perspective. All I can usefully do is flag up the bias. Much of what is offered as specific in this book can be taken purely as examples. I talk about myself because it's a way of exploring the underlying theme of how we create our stories. It is in no way meant to suggest that my take on Druidry, or my ancestry, is in any way definitive, nor to denigrate anyone else's experience. This is simply the material I have to work with. I think this means most readers will have to bring some creative engagement to the book. When considering any of the issues I raise, please substitute your own stories for mine as far as possible. I offer mine as a model so that I'm not talking in cold abstracts all the time.

Of course I have an agenda. No one sits down to write a book devoid of opinions and free from intentions, and I would be prepared to bet that if anyone did, the book itself would be agonizingly dull! Do I want to spell my agenda out right now so that we all know where we stand? Of course not. It would be like telling you the punch line before offering the actual joke. I want to persuade you, and take you on a journey that will encourage you to view things in certain ways. This would be true of most authors, to some degree at least.

Do I fully know what my agenda is? Do I embark upon this book fully conscious of all the pressures, influences, beliefs and assumptions now acting upon me? I doubt anyone knows that when they set out to write, or to do anything else. I could offer you a full and detailed history of me and take up half the book with it, and there are no guarantees it would better equip you the reader to properly assess the usefulness of my words, or to set me in my proper context. As was hammered into us in my days of studying English literature 'the design or intention of the author is neither available nor desirable as a standard for judging the success of a work of literary art.'[11] I can't tell you, and it might not even help if I did.

I'm offering myself as a working example now, because all story-making is human. Everyone who has ever taken a stab at recording, investigating or commenting on history, has also been a person. They've had reasons for considering certain issues. Often they've had wider political, or social points to make. Whether we can guess their bias or motivation varies.

It is often said that history is written by the winners. We need to expand that definition. History is written by the educated, and where it is based on written evidence, it is based on the evidence of those wealthy and educated enough to leave a written record. This means that for much of history, women and the poor have left little direct evidence of their own thoughts, feelings and beliefs. Much writing has been in the hands of a male elite, and the Church. We know of those outside this sphere mostly through the comments made by those within it, with all the inherent biases and misunderstandings that can bring. What few written 'voices' there are for the many silent people, may be erroneously mistaken for a representation of the whole.

Writing on the English Revolution, Stevie Davies observes, 'Most women continued to eke a subsistence in poverty and illiteracy, bound in to the cycle of toil, child-bearing, child-burial and widowhood: they register in history as silence. Eerily, I was aware of this mass silence as I listened to the few voices that could make themselves heard.'[12] Edward Vallance makes a parallel observation about the Peasant's revolt of the 1300s. 'The previous silence of the historical record, as far as the voice of ordinary people was concerned, was replaced by a deafening roar.'[13] Most of our ancestors are part of the historical silence.

As soon as we try to contemplate the past, we have to give up much hope of finding just the certainty of hard facts and reconcile ourselves to spending some of the time wading through the sludge created by other people's beliefs, assumptions and intentions. Stuart Piggott points out that we must 'endeavor to detect where concepts and motifs have been unconsciously imposed on the Druids by those who first wrote about them.'[14] But this imposition is not limited to the distant past, or for that matter, to Druidry.

Not least, there is the problem for readers that every last author wants you to believe that they have authority. The clue was always there, in the name. Every author wants you to trust them, and to accept their version of things. When it comes to writing about spiritual 'truth' as history, there may be a demand inherent in the text to accept everything you are reading as Right. Perhaps even to believe that the author was God. Many authors present similar, non-god-based attitudes to the inherent validity of other kinds of truth, too. The authority of 'evidence' can be used as a justification for all manner of things, even when no evidence is offered, or vast conclusions spring wildly from small fragments of knowledge.

My understanding is that authors are not god, in any circumstance, and that all human experience is recorded by humans and subject to all the many things humans do to stories. The most influential feature of story-making is that we try to get the narrative into coherent shapes that make sense and mean something. This is why stories are not like life – which is messy and often appears to mean very little. In trying to make history make sense, we are of necessity focusing on certain narrative lines, limited by what we have detailed information about, obliged to extrapolate, and trying to clarify things that might not have simple explanations. The more we push towards clear and simple narratives, the more risk we run of getting things wrong. The details tend to matter, and simplicity tends to skip over them, ignores the bits that don't fit, and otherwise reduces things down.

Story-making can focus history in a number of ways. We may tell the tale through the life of a few individuals, or by responding to those few who showed up in written record. This can create a distorting effect, over-emphasizing the importance of those we focus on. We might pick a specific time, or a movement, to create a narrative thread. This can miss out aspects of continuity that become visible with a bigger context. It can create a misleading perspective of events. For example apparent Roman horror over Celtic human sacrifice stands considering in the context of the gladiatorial arena and crucifixion. The Romans were not kind, as a people, but their own methods and reasons for killing were familiar, while those of any 'barbarian' race were not and would therefore be considered differently. Our own relationship with a behavior informs how we see it. That which we do, we will see in a different way to something we have never done. This can create distorting shapes when we come to fit the past into narratives.

There are, I think, two dominating forces in narratives about human history as well as a number of other story themes that can be fitted around them. There is the story of progress, and the story of decay. They have been with us for a long time. I am not sure of their age, but both manifest noticeably in Victorian writing. The celebration of progress in both technology and humanity very much features in a post industrial revolution world. Technology was developing at a startling pace and the belief that it, and human ingenuity, would pave the way to all manner of great things, was very much part of a Victorian worldview. At least it was for those well enough off to reap the benefits of 'progress'. I imagine that for slum dwellers facing a decline in standards of living, the picture looked rather different. Decay narratives become very apparent around the 1890s, with a rush of anxiety about the potential degradation of humanity. The calendar date may have been an influence, the new century looming, but there was also the influence of Darwin, and less certainty about the exalted status of humanity (and especially the English) in the great scheme of things.

Even then, decay was not a new idea. Consider the golden era of ancient Greece, replaced by epochs that were never as good as the one that went before it. I gather that ancient Chinese history contains a similar thought form. Stuart Piggott quotes classical author Strabo commenting on 'an original life of simplicity and virtue, from which we ourselves have lamentably declined.'[15] The idea of decay is there in the Old Testament too, with the perfection of Eden replaced by something inferior. Whenever we talk about 'Golden Age' it's always something in the past, the era of greatness we do not think will come again. Around the time of the English Civil War, people were preparing for the end of the world, in a literal way, in anticipation that Jesus would be leading an army. Oliver Cromwell must have been a considerable anticlimax.

When we pick an overarching narrative about the shape of history, we may say more about ourselves than we do about the past. It is important to be clear that historians are story-makers, and no matter how objective they may claim to be, they are human and as open to unconscious influences as anyone else.

They may also be consciously motivated to interpret information in certain ways. There is nothing original in my observing this. According to a text on the Iron Age from the British Museum,

> *We do not discover history. We identify evidence and then create history, using the fragments of surviving information, and our understanding of the contemporary world and human societies, to make narratives and explanations of what we think happened. Consequently, histories inevitably reflect the preoccupations, preconceptions and blind-spots of the people and times which produced them.*[16]

Offering a more detailed example of how this works in practice, Edward Vallance observes that for some historians, 'Leveller ideas only appear 'modern' when viewed through the distorting lens of a Marxist/Socialist historiography that wishes to place them with a 'tradition' of British radicalism.'[17] He then goes on to point out that the Levellers were not considered at all important to previous historians considering the period. So were earlier historians biased against the more socialist nature of the Leveller movement, or were later historians biased by a desire to find evidence of proto-socialism? Interestingly, Vallance himself pays no attention to the role of women within the Leveller movement, something only more overtly feminist authors have tended to pick up on. It may be the case that we tend to see the things we went looking for, and miss the aspects that do not resonate with us.

Stevie Davies, again, comments on the work of historian Christopher Hill who 'all but censored out, unread, women of the caliber of Cary, Trapnel and Fell. Women were presented as Ranter sex objects, in a web of witty anecdote. Political issues, as they related to women, were likewise obscured.'[18] For those who are not looking for women as active contributors to history, women in history have just not existed. That 'women's history' has been taught as a distinct subject, speaks volumes about its previous and, arguably, continuing absence from the mainstream.

Historians are inevitably a product of their time and place and able to reflect only the level of understanding available to them. They must see the past through the eyes of the present. New technological and scientific developments keep coming along to cast old thinking in a new light. Philosophy, religion and politics all influence the interpretation of history and help determine what deserves attention and what does not. Traditional 'history' focused on the actions of the ruling elite and misses out the lives of the vast majority of people who pass unremarked. The majority of human experience is not recorded for posterity, the influences of so many lives left unexplored. Yet for most of us, these small, unnoticed stories are far more relevant, for being far closer to what we can expect for ourselves.

When we think about those antiquarian ancestors of Druidry, this is hugely significant. They operated in a world in which the Old Testament was literal truth. The world had only existed for a few thousand years, so far as they knew, so ascribing ancient sites to more recent peoples made total sense. They didn't have carbon dating, and they were inventing the discipline and sciences that would later be able to establish where they'd gone wrong. An honorable worker with insufficient tools and abundant misinformation is unlikely to get everything right. However, too many books, and too much thinking still depend on this very distorted perspective of history. Reclaiming the pagan past in a way that is accurate and usefully available is an epic work in progress, one continually hindered by fantasy and the regurgitation of old mistakes.

History as progress

The story of progress currently draws inspiration from evolution and the idea that things improve, becoming the fittest, and assuming the optimal forms. The story is older than ideas of evolution though. It usually positions humanity at the very pinnacle; representing the best that evolution or history can achieve. Thus we are superior to our ancestors, and to all other living things. Furthermore, human cultural history can be a narrative of progress, going from the ignorant, barbaric past to the enlightened, improved and civilized present. This is a version based on my own, western world view and may not have the same shape in other places.

This story of history has a number of consequences. First it reinforces the idea of human superiority present in monotheistic religions. It can easily replace god with evolution as an explanation for this superiority, but it is a mistaken claim. Evolution does not move towards pinnacles of excellence, but instead is all about adaption for the current circumstances. As temperatures, weather, sea levels and other pressures change, so does 'best' for the environment. Evolution does not create an easy, linear story of life forms growing towards ever greater achievement. The ancestors of whales clambered out of the sea to become mammals, and then for some reason, went back to the waters to develop the whale form we now see. This is not progress towards a goal, but ongoing change.

The second issue of the progress narrative is that, having accepted it, everything that we do can readily be defined as progress over what went before. Technology, industrialization, urbanization and development are all 'progress', even when, as with Victorian slum dwellers, this is evidently not the case. The narrative of progress does not encourage us to ask what we might have lost along the way, or to question what progress costs. It also assumes that we must keep heading forwards, onwards and upwards into the ever brighter, shinier future. It is a narrative that can therefore be used to justify any form of replacing the old with the new.

The progress narrative often makes the present into the

endpoint previous history was aiming for. That which got us to here represents progress, and anything that stood in the way of said, was counterproductive. This is not an inevitable consequence of the progress narrative, but is one that has been associated with it, and with a significant body of historical writing.

> It is part and parcel of the whig interpretation of history that it studied the past with reference to the present; and though there may be a sense in which this is unobjectionable if its implications are carefully considered, and there may be a sense in which it is inescapable, it has often been an obstruction of historical understanding because it has been taken to mean the study of the past with direct and perpetual reference to the present.[19]

In The Whig Interpretation of History, author Herbert Butterfield calls upon historians to study the past for its own sake, and to seek to make sense of it on its own terms, rather than to use it to prop up the present status quo. This raises some important ideas for the maker of historical stories: Are we exploring the past for its own sake, or because we mean to utilize it in some way? The ways in which we make use of history can so easily influence the ways in which we interpret it.

When we focus on the present and look to see how the past got us here, we miss all the detours, doubling back, conflict and uncertainty that combine to create actual life. We simplify the narrative into a bold, straight line that pushes onwards. We may then wonder why things aren't so clear cut and driven in our own age. We may also miss the ways in which the subplots and counter stories influence the main action.

History as decay

The second narrative postulates a past in which everything was better, cleaner, more honest, healthier, happier and otherwise an improvement, from which humans have degenerated. This manifests in a number of ways. For religious fundamentalists, it tends to mean the idea that we started out perfect in God's image, we fell from grace and we've got to work our way out of it. For pagans it often means the idea of a perfect, matrilineal, goddess worshipping society full of peace, love, tolerance and goodness, which has since been over-run by the interconnected evils of patriarchy and capitalism. For our Victorian ancestors, decay was not just a moral issue, but also a physical one, which gives us tales like The Time Machine, full of fear for future human degeneration.

While the history-as-progress narrative has a simple future projection in the form of 'more progress' the decay narrative is more complicated. The decay story calls on us to go backwards. It demands that we construct the future by returning to the values of that other, better time (whenever that is imagined to have been). We go back to a purer version of the faith, a more authentic translation of the text, a better set of laws, and a more demanding set of moral guidelines. The periods pointed to and the remedies recommended vary considerably. The only consistency is that the past was, at some point, a better place and the only way forward is back. Then we might get it right. Interestingly, the model of decay assumes that once we go back to the 'magic' period, we can then shift into the narrative of progress instead, frequently taking with us the chosen few who have done the right thing, and finally leaving the degenerates behind.

The progress model at least has the advantage of being able to embrace everyone, while the decay model tends to feature a set of people who represent all the degeneration we need to get away from and who should therefore be pushed out. In the progress model, history is used to illustrate how bad things used to be, to point out how far we've come and to reinforce the idea that we need to keep plugging away in the right direction. The decay version uses history to reinforce its assertions about where it thinks we are going wrong. Both of them depend entirely on the individual's subjective understanding of the past and their definition of 'better'.

The narrative of history seems like a far more complex, ambiguous thing to me, but that doesn't lend itself to neat sound bites or a good rallying cry. I think many of us would agree that we like our indoor plumbing, health care, hot and cold flowing electricity, freedom of speech and movement. Many of us have far more options, a far longer life expectancy and far more material comfort than our ancestors. But does that make us happier? We will probably never know. What research there is does seem to suggest that for all the extra toys, we probably aren't any happier after all.[20]

I would like the pre-industrial revolution levels of pollution, the lack of noise pollution and light pollution from the past. I'd like back the creatures we've lost – aurochs especially. Maybe not anything from before the last ice age though. I'd like to wind back the clock on everything our species has got wrong whilst keeping all the bits I like, to do with communications, hot running water, human rights laws, trains, and Quorn, just to pick a random selection. There is no perfect period that's going to give me aurochs and Quorn on the same afternoon. I want the minimal ownership ethos of nomadic hunter gatherers, but I still want internet access. Progress in the conventional sense cannot give me this, nor can any fantasy of somehow going backwards to recapture what I might imagine we have lost.

During my teens I went through a period of imagining that pre-industrial life was so much better than the modern age, and daydreaming about the kind of apocalypse that could magically put the clock back. Fantasy and science fiction stories are riddled with the same premise, so I at least have the consolation of knowing it wasn't just me. Periods of apocalyptic thinking have cropped up at different times and places in human history, sometimes prompted by calendar dates, as with the 2012 phenomena, sometimes brought on by conflict. An approaching apocalypse, or at least the belief in one, can make sense of the impossible, and give meaning to horror and fear that make it possible to cope with life. 'The worse things are, the better. The inscrutable welter of history becomes a meaningful code.'[21]

When everything in the world seems wrong it can be tempting to imagine that we must tear everything down and start again. A nice, big apocalypse would be a quick and neat way of doing this, after which we'll have the freedom to set up our perfect world. It's lazy thinking, really, because it avoids working out how we get there from here in any real sense. If all we did was fail to imagine how to make progress, the fantasies of decay would not be so much of a problem. Unfortunately, there are people who want to build their brave new world and don't seem at all averse to the idea of blowing up the one we've got. Real change has to be built, carefully, from within. An apocalypse might make a good film plot, but is no way to achieve anything.

I think the mental process underpinning the progress model is fairly simple. I think it's also very flawed, because it assumes that new things are invariably better than old things, that we are going somewhere, and that we will keep heading the right way so long as we keep producing and inventing. Science will find the solution. I'm not sure it will. But as an idea it's easy to see why people might choose to believe it – this is a take that fits perfectly with the drive of capitalism, the emphasis on economic growth, and the narrative of scientific advance.

The progress model sits squarely in the mainstream, justifying political decisions and encouraging us not to look at the costs. Currently, the decay model often belongs to the fringes – to religious fundamentalists, and also to other people who find themselves dissatisfied by modern life – some of whom are fairly mainstream conservatives. It's easy to romanticize the past, to envisage it as a Pre-Raphaelite painting, skipping over the mud, plague and child mortality. We ignore the details that don't fit, safe in the knowledge that, as we can't have the past back, we can harp on about it at no personal risk. Plenty of dystopian fiction explores what happens when our perfect past is resurrected, and it seldom turns out to be pretty.

Is the desire for improvement inherent in the human condition? Are we innately unable to accept what we have and obliged to strive after more? I don't know. Some of us seem more afflicted by this urge than others. It breeds dissatisfaction but it also inspires innovation.

History as continuity

The narratives of progress and decline both depend on the idea of change, taking humanity in a specific direction and for a definite purpose. Any historical narrative focusing on change will skim over the issues of continuity. I suppose a focus on continuity in mundane things would not make for a very dynamic and engaging work, and that may in itself explain some part of it.

However, when it comes to English literature as a discipline, one of the key ideas students have to consider is whether human emotion is consistent over time. When Shakespeare talks about love, duty and jealousy, does he mean things that we too feel in the same ways, or is there something else going on? In practice, when we are readers of stories and audiences of plays, we are assuming that not much has changed. The rage or despair of an ancient Greek figure is just the same as our rage and despair, or we can't hope to understand the story. Every time we engage with a work of contemporarily created fiction or film set in the past, we return to the basic assumption that when it comes to emotions and thought processes, there are constants we can rely on. The costume and technology might change, but passions are all the same.

This is a notion that explorers of history and ancestry also need to consider. Herbert Butterfield observes, 'The primary assumption of all attempts to understand the men of the past must be the belief that we can in some degree enter into minds that are unlike our own.'[22] However, Stuart Piggott holds the opposing view: 'It is a waste of time thinking that we can enter the minds and share the psychological and emotional states of the early Celts.'[23]

The assumption of emotional continuity might not stand up to much scrutiny. Life experiences shape our sense of proportion. The further back you go, the more common infant mortality becomes, for example. For modern parents, this is a life shattering tragedy. But if you could be sure of losing at least one child, if you had lost siblings, cousins and neighbors as children, would you relate to the death of a child in the same way? Grief visible in written accounts from the past seems palpable. Historical people saw far more of death than we moderns do, can we be certain that our understanding of it is commensurate with theirs? The grotesque death images sometimes associated with mediaeval graves suggest a wholly different attitude to modern squeamishness about mortality and decay. The complex Victorian etiquette of grieving suggests a culture somewhat obsessed with mortality. We do things very differently now, so can we possibly feel exactly the same way?

We know perfectly well that different historical periods have had different philosophies. We also know that intellect and emotion are not wholly unrelated. The whole premise underlying Cognitive Behavioral Therapy – popular for tackling anxiety, depression and obsessive compulsive behaviors – is that changing how you think about a thing will change how you feel. And yet one of the most enduring ideas we have about history, is that people can be assumed to feel in the same sorts of ways, no matter what the prevailing philosophy of the time may have had them thinking. How people feel informs their behavior. Thought, feeling and action are all known to be related. Change one and you change the others. And yet we still assume human emotion to be a constant over time.

The modern romance genre is peppered with awful historical fiction in which heroines with twenty first century sensibilities do and say the kinds of things that most women historically simply would not have done. Romance fiction is full of modern feminism and education foisted onto women who were not legally allowed to own property and who existed during times when there was no such thing a rape within marriage, for example. Rare is the novelist like Elizabeth Chadwick who really does consider how those different philosophical approaches might inform the emotional lives of the characters. Thinking and feeling are not entirely separate activities. Yet fiction suggests we are generally very happy to accept that you can have foreign thoughts and familiar emotions. Every science fiction romance between a strange, alien being and some regular human goes to reinforce the idea.

On the flip side, there are other kinds of continuity that are referred to in passing. Farming tools and the lives of the poor have not changed a vast amount through much of history. The garb of a Saxon peasant and a mediaeval one have more in common than not – some kind of trousers, some kind of tunic for the men, a long, simple dress for the women. Plowing and reaping didn't change a vast amount between the Iron Age and industrialization. Nations may rise and fall, but for the people making the bread, the story of harvest, grinding, kneading and baking will have been much the same. The narrative of progress talks about the new wonders of industrialization, but does not often linger over the price poor people paid for it, in slums, ill health, industrial injury, loss of way of life, whilst they did not reap many of the benefits of 'progress'.

Folk history offers a different perspective to wealth creation and progress. 'We're not too low to weave the cloth but we're too low the cloth to wear!'[24]

Change makes for story, where continuity does not. But in our own lives, we may well be far more influenced by continuity than by change. Change is easy to spot, it has its inherent drama and so we pay attention to it. That which continues unbroken, is merely normal, and goes unchallenged.

If we believe that change is good and inherently makes things better, we embrace a world view that will reject old ways of doing things simply because they are old. 'New and improved' remains a favorite marketing slogan. Although how a thing can be both simultaneously, I am unsure. New is allegedly good, but love is ancient, also allegedly. These are all stories, not facts, and as such are all open to challenge.

The other side to the continuity story comes from a desire to establish a thread, holding different movements or people together. By establishing continuity, we claim, or imagine we claim, the authenticity of age. Thus radical thinkers have sometimes tried to paint a picture of unbroken radical action in the UK. 'When radical activity appeared non-existent, it had simply gone underground, only to resurface, its fundamental nature intact in another epoch.'[25] This is very much a parallel of the efforts gone to, creating narratives of continuance for pagan traditions. It's part of a desire to belong, to own a narrative that places current action in a meaningful context. Being a radical, or a pagan, or any other kind of transgression from normality, can feel very lonely indeed. Belonging to a tradition gives a tribe, even if all its other members are long since dead. The comfort this offers can encourage us to see unbroken continuity that probably isn't there.

History as change

The past is a foreign country: they do things differently there.[26]

It is possible to have narratives of change without there being a clear direction for the change to be taking us. We can simply identify the past as 'other' without requiring it to be part of a journey towards betterment or decline. In many ways, this makes a lot of sense – most of history is beyond our personal experience. It is separate from us. There are a number of ways in which we can work with this kind of story, and the impact of it as a view depends considerably on how and why we deploy it.

Firstly in taking the past as 'other' we can then choose to view it as irrelevant. Other times, other peoples, societies, religions and cultures have no bearing on us. They were then, and different, we are now and entirely our own thing. By emphasizing the narrative of change and difference, we can also play down the relevance of history for our current lives. I'm more of the opinion that those who do not learn from history are condemned to repeat it and, from that perspective, I find the rejection of history to be a misguided, short sighted and self-deluding approach.

In literature, the figure of the 'other' is often used to help define the characters we are meant to identify with. The 'other' is all that we, or the lead character, are not, and through the contrast, we know ourselves, and can express identity. It is easy to employ narratives about history in this way, using it to emphasize the current traits that we value in ourselves, individually or culturally. This may be tied in to narratives about progress, but that angle does not need to be made explicit. We might not see the journey as one of sustained progress from the 'bad old days' to here, but one of deliberate, conscious upheaval as a younger, better generation has dramatically rejected a previous way of being. So we might choose to see radical change in the narrative of female emancipation, rather than exploring the evolution of gender roles, or the continuity between the lives of working women past and present, for example.

We may also associate the modern behavior of 'others' with the 'otherness' of history. The most obvious example here would be the equating of contemporary indigenous people with the primitive ancestors of Europe – a popular theme for colonialists. If we equate a modern state, or group of people with something in our own history, we can use that to point out how far behind us they are. It might also make us uncomfortable about our own origins but I think that's a secondary issue. Again this is not a new way of thinking. As far as I can tell, Roman writers characterized those around them as 'barbarians' and many more recent scholars have been happy to take that assessment on trust. Piggott writing in the late sixties was evidently comfortable talking about 'primitive' people and how we view them, and comparing more and less 'advanced' peoples. It's not always easy to tell if the attitudes rightfully belong to the modern writer or the older writer they are ascribed to – not having access to the originals makes this harder.

We do this as much as anything else to tell ourselves about our own superiority. It is a narrative that helps us evade responsibility, if we are not careful with it. If we employ it on a personal level – assessing someone as being at a life stage we have long since passed through, we might affirm our own right to authority over them based on the idea that we are more advanced, and therefore superior. To accuse someone of living in the past, or being 'so last century' is to make explicit that we see them as inferior. In doing this, we pass up opportunities to scrutinize our own lives, all issues of manners aside.

History as invasion

Back when I went through school, there was a tendency to teach British history as being one of invasion. While this is no longer the prevailing thought form in modern history books, there are plenty of older books still floating about out there, waiting to mislead the unsuspecting reader.

Invasion theory goes like this: New and superior peoples come in from somewhere, bringing innovation and technology with them. In this interpretation, any radical new development becomes evidence of invasion. When we are dealing with the murky realms of pre-history, with only artifacts to guide us, those objects inevitably get priority in how we understand things. A new art form sweeping across Europe, a new funeral rite, or house building style, has to have spread by some means, and for a long time invasion was the story used to explain this.

Ronald Hutton, in The Prehistoric Religions of the British Isles written in 1991, pointed out that historians are moving away from ideas of invasion towards recognition that cultures could fall apart from stresses within them, and that new goods could represent the buying of prestige items, not a movement of individuals.[27] Why have we been so quick to assume that change means new people? It also begs the question of where all these 'new people' are supposed to have come from. If every country interprets change as signifying invasion, there's nowhere for the new forms or ideas to begin. Logically, each new way of doing things began somewhere, unless we want to believe that each shift in art and funeral is proof of contact with alien races. I think not.

This narrative is especially resonant when we think about ancient Druid ancestry. Were the Celts a mobile, invasive people or did Celtic culture develop naturally out of what went before it, spread by trade and other friendly forms of contact? There is a theory that the 'Celtic peoples' were invaders coming to Britain from the European continent. It is the placing of Druids in an invading Celtic context that rules out the idea that they descended from the people who built Stonehenge and other such sites. However, it is the continuation of 'Celtic cultures' in Wales, Scotland, Ireland and France that have also justified claims of a survival of Druidry, in bardic traditions, folklore and secret societies. Do we view the ancient Druids as part of a continental Celtic invasion, or as part of a much older native tradition?

The narrative of progress through invasions by superior

peoples makes a lot more sense when you put it in context of the times in which these ideas emerged. Archaeology has its beginnings in the late seventeenth century although it has evolved a good deal since then. It began as a discipline, in England at the time when the country was a significant colonial power, and its early development coincides with advancing colonialism. European countries of the time were out claiming pieces of the world for themselves. Those recording history in other parts of the world were more likely than not to be from a white colonial background. The idea that progress comes as a result of invasion by superior races is perfectly logical in this context, and serves to uphold the beliefs of the time, which makes me think this is what's underpinning the idea. If ancient progress depended on invasion, then history justifies colonialism as a natural route to the improvement of all peoples. For colonizers, it is such an obvious, convenient narrative that there would be no reason to challenge it. But that doesn't make the story accurate, nor should it hide the fact that this is simply one interpretation of data, not the only one available.

Currently we seem more interested in narratives of integration, of trade distributing ideas and styles. This again is consistent with our times, and the priority we now give to market forces. Who knows what narratives future generations may bring to their image of history?

History as innovation

The book religions tend towards an idea of progress being dependent on divine revelation. It is through the word of God (whichever god you happen to believe in) that society gets its laws, values and early civilizing developments. As the invasion narrative demonstrates, we are reluctant to view progress as happening inherently, and are often more willing to seek external sources. There are plenty of New Age folk who believe that all pagan wisdom came from Atlantis, and that the

Atlanteans in turn came from another world, or were taught by aliens. Apparently a lot of us prefer to think of wisdom as coming from somewhere else.

The study of folklore in its early days was underpinned by the idea that folk traditions contained elements of much earlier cultures, perhaps even remnants of ancient pagan belief. No one gave much attention to the idea that they may have been recently made up. Folk is a living, breathing tradition and comes up with new things all the time. Age and authenticity are not entirely the same things. While it's known (but not by me until very recently) that there are standard forms used by Roman writers, that's not usually considered much in terms of Druid representations. The obligatory big speeches put words into the mouths of protagonists. Nuances of language might have reflected literary inclinations, not factual accuracy. The use of stock-phrases may mean Druids being characterized in ways that were more about literary habit than reality. The necessity of including some ethnographic content in histories may cast Caesar's writing in a different light.[28] By not considering the literary innovations of Roman writers, and taking them as straight, factual depictions, we may be doing the equivalent of taking Shakespeare's history plays as a factual basis for understanding English history.

Why are we so keen to reject the idea of our own capacity to innovate? This one perplexes me. The social upheavals of the late sixteen hundreds saw huge innovation and dramatic, unprecedented changes in the UK, including civil war and the beheading of King Charles the First. The very time at which ancient history and archaeology were emerging as disciplines was the time at which the capacity for human dramatic change based solely on human creativity was massively visible. And yet the idea of historical innovation was not as popular as narratives that either rooted ancient wisdom in the Bible, or sought to migrate it around the classical world. Was this some kind of reaction to the dynamic changes of the time? Did ancient history become interesting to people precisely because the changes they were living through had a destabilizing effect? I can only speculate.

It is entirely possible to interpret classical writing on the Druids as showing that Druidry developed in Britain and that the British Isles remained its hub and central teaching place. In other words, the ancient British came up with it all by themselves, with no reference to anyone else. Yet it appears that once the likes of Aubrey and Toland, Stukely and all their many followers became interested in Druids, everyone wanted to place the source of that knowledge somewhere else; either in the classical world with Pythagoras, or in the transmission of Biblical knowledge, or perhaps via the Phoenicians. Alternatively, those Iron Age Druids might have been inheritors of older wisdom from previous cultures, or (later) Atlantis. There's a curious absence of enthusiasm for the idea that the whole thing may have been cooked up in the UK by the ancient British themselves.

There has been an equally curious reluctance in some quarters to admit that modern Druidry might have been entirely created by modern Druids, working from the inspiration of Aubrey and Stukely, down through Iolo Morganwg, Reid, and other curious and creative figures to those who are inventing and re-inventing today.

Asking why a thing is a certain way, is a very natural impulse. I believe children do so universally, where they have any scope for communication. We ask why things are like this, how they came to be so, and where they came from. The idea that things come from somewhere else; that they have a non-human origin, or a non-human creator, perhaps derives from the longstanding hold of the Bible on our cultures. The history of ascribing human actions to divine influence – from the creation of sacred texts onwards, creates a bias to look outside ourselves for reasons.

One of the questions an author most frequently hears is 'where do you get your ideas from?' We seem to believe as a culture, that ideas, by their very nature, come from somewhere –

specifically, somewhere else. The notion that anyone could explain where an idea came from, and pinpoint it externally, is an odd one, when you stop to look at it. We are reluctant to admit our own capacity for innovating. If our good deeds belong to God and our misdemeanors can be laid on Satan, why bother to think about human ingenuity at all? I have no idea how this relates to perceptions held by non-Christian-influenced countries.

My understanding of humanity, and human history, does not particularly call for any kind of god-presence. I believe that we have written our own religious books and created our own social structures. We may have claimed they were inspired by gods – but people wrote them down and interpreted them, at the very least. I believe that all the things we have historically ascribed to divinity should instead be ascribed to human activity. One of the consequences is that I do not think we always need to be looking somewhere else for explanations.

Thus far I've talked a great deal about history and ancestry, as though those forces make and define everything we might do. This is not my actual belief. I think that history informs us in many ways, shaping our thoughts, intentions and preoccupations. I also think that any one of us, contemporary or historical, has always had the option to reject these legacies and strike out in new directions. I believe fundamentally in the capacity of humans to innovate, to create new things, and to invent whole new ways of understanding the world.

When it comes to modern Druidry, the idea of history as innovation is tremendously important. Not only in terms of how we view our own ancestors of tradition, but for how we imagine ourselves in the present, and where we imagine our fledgling tradition is going. This is a theme I will be returning to.

Good-and-evil stories

If we take the idea that history is progress, then our yardstick for measuring where history progresses to, is inevitably colored by our own time. It is easy to go from the idea of history as progress to the idea that the things in history that brought us to the present moment were the important ones. People whose opinions in the past correspond to the state of the present – or at least to the bits we like about the present, can be perceived heroes, who were ahead of their time, bringing about the changes.

Those who do not support the march of progress can equally be denigrated as reactionary, living in the past, oppressors, misguided and so forth. It is all too easy to disregard the context that made sense of their beliefs, and to ignore the way in which their role in past events contributed to shaping what we have. This focus on progressing to the glorious 'now' can distort how we understand the past, making the present the only measure we care about.

From this understanding it is easy to evolve the story so that those who have supported progress (by our measure of it) were good, while those who opposed it were bad. Valid views that did not turn out to contribute much to modern lives are discarded again, their worthlessness having been clearly established in our minds. By doing this, we reduce our own scope to understand, fashioning a story that validates where we are and makes it harder to question the status quo.

Looking back at the past allows us to make moral judgments that have little bearing on perceptions of people at the time and to then assume these are clear-cut lessons to be learned.

It seems to be assumed that in history we can have something more than the private points of view of particular historians; that there are 'verdicts of history' and that history itself, considered imper-sonally, has something to say to men.[29]

Once again this is about the difference between fact and interpre-tation. It's also, again, an issue more likely to come up with older books and pop-history, where value judgments can be offered as facts. For example, value judgments made by historical authors about early pagans have hugely colored popular understandings of paganism. If the British Museum states as fact that a dead man from the past was murdered by Druids, it is making value a judgment and interpretation, but offering it in a way that an uncritical reader can easily mistake for indisputable truth. These days we expect to have a trial and a jury before we issue such judgments on anyone. A little evidence would not go amiss.

I think for pagans this raises another significant issue. When we consider our own history and the events that have brought us to our current circumstances, it is easy to focus on the change, and the progress. We might tell ourselves that bad old Christian reactionaries suppressed the valiant progressive spiritual movement that finally broke free to allow new age and pagan religions to flourish. If we think that way, we will never explore the often subtle and complex interplay between Christianity and folk magic, or be able to make peace with our own non-pagan ancestors. If we let the stories of our origins and emergence get too colored by who we think we are and what we think we've achieved... the damage we might do ourselves and our cause is considerable. We need to tell our stories from our own perspective and in ways that are resonant for us, just as all peoples do. At the same time, if we want to build something other than flimsy myths, we need to keep our relationship with 'regular' history good. We also need to be able to challenge mainstream history when it represents other people's assumptions as unassailable truth.

Tales of the tides

Come the moment, come the man, as the saying goes.

There is a sense in some historical writing, perhaps unintentional, that history has its own flows and tides. Prevailing beliefs, cultural developments, social changes – all the effects of many unremarked lives moving tiny steps in the same direction. The sum and total of everyone present creates a climate, a circumstance. Then the right person steps forward, takes the lead, breaks through with an innovation, and the tide picks him up and carries him forward. It's almost always a 'him'.

Part of what I like about tidal stories, is that they recognize the existence of all the individuals history otherwise tends to ignore. All those non-famous, marginally influential people who contribute to the zeitgeist, whose momentum can shake the foundations of civilization, make revolution and generate radical change. All they need is the right person at the front, and the tide of history is ready to sweep everything away and make anew.

This is a way of writing about the past that has a rather curious side effect. It may be entirely to do with language. Once you say 'there was a tide of feeling' or anything that suggests that history is just waiting for the right person to step up and get things moving, history becomes a person. History has intentions, an agenda, a willingness to be led one way or another. Either it's a responsive thing offering its harness to anyone with a good idea, or history has a mind of its own and is busy setting up suitable people to take things forward in the right way.

Tide stories are not the most rational way of thinking about history, although it works as a metaphorical way of expressing the multiplicity of individual influences. From a pagan perspective, the idea that history could have tides has a certain appeal. It is a story form that leaves room for ideas of deity, or other non-human agencies such as fate or pre-destination. It allows space for all of us, perhaps, to play a role in the way in which history unfolds. It may, for good or ill, serve to reduce the perceived impact of individual action and creates an impression that things were perhaps inevitable, or meant to be. This could be taken as consistent with a mechanistic view of human behavior, which can tend towards ideas of inevitability, or it can be seen as irrational in some decidedly interesting ways.

Stories about social structures

Once we enter the realms of pre-history, we can only infer from physical remains how people lived and their societies functioned. As only certain kinds of items do not perish over time, we do not even have a full selection of physical remnants to work with. As things currently stand, a single new site containing unexpected finds could potentially re-write our entire understanding of pre-historic life. This demonstrates how fragile and uncertain our stories are.

One of the things we may create narratives about is the social structures people lived in. To do this, we are most likely to match available evidence against known structures. These are ways of thinking that call upon ideas of continuity, and a lack of innovation. We tend to assume that the kinds of groupings and structures favored by the ancients will have something in common with the kinds of social structures we know about. To imagine something entirely different would be difficult, and there would not necessarily be any good evidence for it. After all, if we know that some people live in a certain way, we know such a method of living is viable, and that our ancestors could have gone in for it. If we imagine whole new structures for them, we may well be creating fantasy.

One of the interesting questions raised by pre-history is whether specialization in terms of tools and the use of resources can be equated to a separating of tasks and an increasing complexity of social structure. To what extent does social structure relate to physical property? And do we equate physical property with ownership, and ownership with power? Our own culture suggests these connections, but does that justify applying them to the past? We often assume that grave goods are sent with the person into their afterlife. However, traditional gypsies, as I understand it, burn a person's possessions with them, not with a view to the afterlife, but because it's not clean to keep things belonging to the dead. Graeme Talboys makes the additional point that, 'Personal items such as jewelry, weapons, professional tools, games and the like all become endowed with the spirit of their owner through prolonged use and close personal contact.'[30] Thus burying items could as easily about laying to rest the extended expressions of the dead person, as it might be a desire to furnish them with items for the afterlife. Just because we know some cultures entombed objects for the afterlife does not mean we should assume all buried goods are evidence of the same belief system.

Humans have perhaps always been social creatures, and to make any narrative sense of human history, we also have to find plausible stories about the societies our ancestors lived in. There are certain things we can infer from the practical evidence and realties. If you are a nomad, you can't own more than you can transport. A settled, agrarian life lends itself more to the ownership of property. We associate that settled, ownership state with a rising warrior elite, leadership and structure. Physical evidence may seem to support this, if, for example, we see the big hut as indicating the presence of a chief. But we may be overlooking the communal gathering place, or a barn, or something else beyond our experience and imaginations. The further back we go from the written resources, the less we know about what structure, if any, existed, and the more we have to assume, or imagine. Inferring from physical remains is possible, but not foolproof, and keeping sight of the inherent uncertainties is very important.

We have a modern elite in the UK whose status is based on physical wealth, and the wealth of their ancestors. The history of that elite has a lot to do with a ruling warrior class. The history of Europe can be described in horribly simplified terms, as clans forming into bigger units, eventually turning into city states and other small states, which then combine through shared language and history to develop larger nations with distinct identities and a ruling elite who owe their success to military prowess, and who continue to control the money and land. This is our underpinning notion of normal human progress, then, moving from the warrior rulers towards more inclusive democracy. Thus the story of progress is the rise of tyrants to their ruling of ever bigger areas of land and ever larger populations, and then the replacement of that with the much better system of democracy.

There are two problems with that story – firstly that wealth and power are still concentrated in a small percentage of the population despite democracy, and secondly that the Greeks, Romans and the Vikings, that we know of, dabbled with forms of democracy. To what extent do we look back at the past through the lenses of current experience?

Some feminist goddess worshippers have a story of the past that includes matrilineal societies ruled over by women. Patriarchy rose up and destroyed that. Socialists and communists can look at our mysterious ancient ancestors and see how it used to be the case that the people held the power and that a ruling elite set themselves up by dint of superior arms, and have been oppressing the workers ever since. Someone with more sympathy for the ruling elite can look back and see that we have always had clans and structures; that we must have always lived under some kind of leadership, that kings and chieftains are both ancient and natural. An anarchist can easily decide that there was a time before we got into all this fixed social structure malarkey. Perhaps the hunter gatherers better understood how to take individual responsibility and to avoid abdicating power to others. And of course we Druids can look back and see how the wise and responsible Druids went round telling people how to do things properly, and we can sigh to ourselves and imagine how much better that must have been as a system.

It's very easy to impose the systems we want onto our understanding of the past and to imagine that our ancestors did all the things we want to be able to do, and hold all the proof we will ever require, that our way is the best way.

Stories about religion

If a find has no obvious practical purpose, or is downright impractical, it will very likely be assumed to have a religious function. Sites that are now understood to be burial places with their coverings and contents long vanished, were once thought to be altars. Art also tends to be understood as religious. For example, consider the ancient figures of rounded female forms known as Venus figurines, which are prehistoric statues between four and twenty five centimeters tall. Most come from Europe in the Upper Paleolithic with the oldest date I've seen at thirty five thousand years ago, making them among the oldest ceramics known. These are widely thought of as goddess images as the 'Venus' title suggests, and not, for example, as stone age pornography. Where cave paintings happen in difficult places, we construct narratives about religious rites, or rites of passage. We don't look around our cities at the unlikely and dangerous spots teenagers clamber to in order to leave their graffiti.

As we don't actually know a great deal about pre-historic religions, we have no means to interpret any potentially religious finds. Or, we have far too much scope. There is a great deal of room into which we can bring our own needs and assumptions, and so little information that it can readily be presented to fit.

When the people writing about ancient Druids were themselves very Christian, they sought ways to interpret what they assumed to be Druid temples, in a Christian context, wanting to harmonize the Druids with their own beliefs. The modern Druidic movement is one of nature worship, tends to be non-dogmatic, and is frequently either polytheistic or animist in outlook. Of course we want the ancient Druids to have been the same. It may be the case, as Graeme Talboys suggests, that 'Druid' is merely an externally imposed name for the Celtic intellectual class and covers all of the professional people, not just the priests. If this is so, then the modern social equivalent of ancient Druidry is a very long way from the lives of most contemporary people who self-identify as Druids.

The whole idea of ancient paganism as fertility cult, which as I understand it is central to modern Wicca, comes originally from Frazer's interpretations in The Golden Bough. It is a construct built by interpreting different religions, old and new, in light of each other, culminating in a theory of vegetable worship and a sacrifice god. In terms of modern pagan thinking, Frazer has been hugely influential, while in terms of academic worth he has long since been discounted. Where does that leave the stories we tell based upon his work?

Archaeologists have never knowingly dug up a Druid. How would they tell if they did? A golden sickle in the grave, perhaps? And so we have the problem that Druidry can only be read into the archaeology from an initial assumption that it is indeed there to be found. The religious meaning of finds can only be interpreted, they cannot speak for themselves, and frequently 'religious' as a tag may just mean 'can't see any sensible use for it'. We see deposits in water as offerings to spirits or gods, and it is being considered that hoards put in the ground may too have been left for religious reasons, but this doesn't tell us what the offerings were *for* exactly. How would we distinguish between a human sacrifice and someone put to death for crime? If the translations and interpretations of classical writers are to be believed, the ancient Druids used criminals as their sacrifices. How clear are the lines between justice and religion? Violent death, as with Lindow Man, has been taken as evidence of sacrifice, but aside from the comments made by classical authors, there is no real reason to do this. If we had no concept of human sacrifice, we wouldn't have interpreted it into the finds.

For example, in 2008 a grave was discovered near Colchester, which was reported as the first Druid grave to be unearthed. '...the find yielded cremated human remains, a board game, medical tools, religious implements and evidence of a psychedelic drink used for divination.'[31] It's the presence of medical tools and religious implements that clinches the impression of Druidry. How do we know we are seeing religious artifacts? Something in the grave was interpreted as being divining rods, but how can we be certain? And note the way in which the psychedelic drink is assumed to mean divination, and not something used medicinally – which would be compatible with those medical tools. Reading in the divinatory meaning means we can now 'know' that the Druids used drugs for divination and that we have not dug up the grave of an Iron Age raver. Circular logic strikes again!

When we go looking for evidence of religion in the remnants left by our pre-historic ancestors, we take with us the assumption that it could be possible to tell the difference between the sacred and the profane. How new an idea is this? We are used to the idea of holy days, sacred places, altars, temples and priests. A religion intrinsic to daily life would be invisible. A religion that had no priesthood, no temples, no books, gave no names to its deities, made no sacrifices – could still function as a religion but wouldn't leave much we could identify.

It's also very easy to claim. Of course there is little evidence of Iron Age Druidry. It was a simple nature religion, the Druids were healers, teachers, they had other roles in the community, they weren't just a priestly elite, they were people called to the spiritual life, like shamans in other cultures. There were no sacrifices, and no books, it was all about learning directly from nature, honoring nature, being outdoors with the elements. It was an instinctive, improvised religion so of course there can be no sound archaeological evidence for it.

And thus I have painted a clear picture of my own, contemporary Druidry, and I've massaged it neatly into pre-history in a way that would be unspeakably difficult to disprove. I wouldn't be the first person to do that, and there is little to stop me trying to pass it off as hard fact and teaching it to others. Except that I won't.

The impact of story

The function of historical narrative is often to engage our present time with the past. We re-imagine based on contemporary understanding, looking for meanings that are relevant now. As a consequence it is very easy for historians, professional or amateur to be caught up in an agenda or interpretation, and explain history in light of that, rather than with any factually based understanding of how things actually happened. I would like to think this is far less of an issue for contemporary academics, but I have no doubt that it has been a significant problem in the past.

An obvious example of this, with far reaching consequences, is the simple belief that primitive peoples are all the same and that what one group does can be used to help explain actions observed in another group, or to help interpret historical cultures. This theory has passed away as an academic one, but I suspect it still exists in plenty of people's minds, and old books are easily bought second hand. However, working with this theory of primitive universalism, Frazer created The Golden Bough. These days its many flaws as both anthropology and history are widely recognized, but the ideas that arose from it have wandered off into the world independent now of the original author, and can turn up in all sorts of unexpected places, offered as 'truth'. Now, to further complicate matters, some authors are reconsidering Frazer, seeing merits in his assessment of the nature of magic, the widespread nature of some practices he observed, the advantages of comparative work and the importance of fertility in folk magic.[32] Picking out the wheat from the chaff becomes ever more challenging.

One of the problems facing a pagan reader who wishes to understand pagan history, is the shortage of good books and the vast array of dross, historical and modern. Ronald Hutton points out that much of the data he shared in his 1991 book The Pagan Religions of the Ancient British Isles, was 'only known so far to specialists.'[33] Much of the modern 'creative' history we have owes a lot to historical misinterpretations. While academia may have quickly discredited Frazer, pagans were a lot slower to cotton on to this. Equally Margaret Murray's influence has been widespread, despite serious academic flaws. The grandfathers of modern archaeology, figures like Toland and Aubrey, wrote about ancient sites, and their ideas are referenced still in all kinds of books and teaching materials. Apparently the methods of writing about history changed in the 1970s[34], when the modern emphasis on considering context and rigorous assessment of sources began. However, how many pagan readers would know to glance at the inside cover for a tell-tale date? And how many books written based on other books, are underpinned by material that has not been critically considered? Again, the interpretations can travel with little reference to the source, and no context for the story being told. Most pagan readers are not historians by training, but are imaginative people with a desire to learn. Finding our own lost history in amongst mainstream publications can consequently be very hard work.

I can speak about this individually. When I first started exploring Druidry, I got a hold of Ross Nichols' book on the subject. I'd heard he was an important figure in the history of OBOD, and he seemed like a serious and credible sort of chap. I struggled with pages on sacred geometry at ancient sites, failed entirely to make any sense of it and gave up. This was not the Druidry I had been looking for. At the time of reading, Nichols seemed to me like a reasonable authority on historical Druidry. Subsequent reading (especially Blood and Mistletoe) places him in a wholly different context for me, and I now feel inclined to reject the whole sacred geometry issue as a preoccupation of people influenced by entirely non-Druidic material. I have a new story, one I am predisposed to keep because it fits so neatly with my own feelings and experiences.

I read a few books on Druidry early on (the titles escape me, for which I can only apologize) but which made clear and definite claims for both the activities and beliefs of ancient Druids. I recall opening a book on Celtic spirituality and being told that to do anything authentic, I must first dedicate myself to learning a Celtic language. Neatly skipping the issue of whether 'Celtic' is a viable term to apply to our Iron Age ancestors, whether modern languages are very akin to Iron Age ones, and whether working in a less familiar language confers any spiritual advantage at all.

Like the majority of modern pagans, I didn't go to the kind of school that teaches ancient Greek and Latin and exposes pupils to classical texts. All of the classical writing on Druids is therefore only available to me in translation, and only those bits other people choose to translate and present as part of their story. Again, I owe a debt to Ronald Hutton here, being the first author I've encountered who has put those quotes into some kind of meaningful context – making it clear that none of the early writing about our Druid ancestors is free from issue, and that all of it is potentially inaccurate. Stuart Piggott's observations on literary forms in Roman texts has also given me pause for thought, making me wonder what, in essence, those texts are.

Again, like the majority of pagans, I am not a trained archaeologist. I manage to keep up with major archaeological events as expressed in the news, but I know nothing of the politics, beliefs and funding pressures informing how modern archaeology does its work. In other words, I have no tools with which to work out how the kinds of stories this discipline creates might relate to my own understanding of the world.

In many ways, paganism is a young and emerging religion, and modern Druidry very much so. Operating in a culture where age of religion is used as proof of validity, where spiritual newness is equated with triviality and insignificance, of course we want stories that position us as old. We want connection with the past, and we want to be validated. My personal belief is that history is never going to give us that.

Having a coherent narrative take on the past can provide people with the drive to act. Whether or not those actions are a good idea is an entirely different question. We can neither prove, nor disprove, any story about the overarching narrative shape of human history. Half an hour with a news program will give you a selection of stories about wondrous progress (scientific, technological, economic, political) and terrible degeneration (obesity, violence, tyranny, falling standards). The idea that life is a dance, one step forward two steps back, shuffle to the side... is not very useful. You can't construct a plan out of something random and unpredictable. If we accept the past as a bit of an amble, we have to consider the idea the future might be the same. If there's no scope for progress, what on earth is the point? And there lies a very interesting question.

Most of us will not do anything that radically affects the course of humanity as a whole. Most of us, like our ancestors, will spend our lives engaged in that dance of forwards, backwards, sideways a bit, shuffle, shuffle, do a little turn. How many of us can look at our own lives and claim any kind of direction there, much less in the wider scheme of things?

If we can look at the enormity of our ancestors and see something other than linear narrative, we can start to reimagine our own lives.

Viewing the ancestors

While our perceptions of history color how we view our ancestors, there are other influences that may be at play. Early anthropologists viewed modern 'primitive' cultures as being comparable to the ancestors of their own 'civilized' nations and there are no doubt still people who hold the same assumptions. Anyone with a desire to empower or romanticize aboriginal peoples will come to the issue of ancestry in a very different way to someone who wishes to establish inferiority.

Our personal politics may come into play here, encouraging

us to view the ancestors as living in greener and more sustainable ways, offering a heroic alternative to our unviable commercial present. We might look back and see the oppression of women, or their liberation, depending on the precise time and culture we care to view.

In deciding the ancestors were inferior, and striving towards the future we have achieved, we might embrace both the idea of progress, and celebrate their good intentions whilst reinforcing the idea that we are better than them. Whatever stories we may decide to tell about our ancestors, we are also telling a story about ourselves. While truth about our ancient ancestors may be scant, the insights into ourselves, as individuals, and our cultures, are much easier to assess on a personal level.

There are a great many stories about who our Druidic ancestors were. By the looks of it, we have been writing stories about them since Roman times. Whether or not any of them are 'true' is hard to say, but if we consider them as narratives, that notion of factual truth is less relevant. These are the myths by which we know ourselves, or are known by others. Rather than offer these in a properly referenced, academic sort of way, I'm going to tell them as little stories, not least because I want to keep visible the story nature of these tales.

Druid story number one

After the flood, one of Noah's sons came to England and taught the locals everything he knew. He blessed them with a very pure version of the one true faith that had been revealed to all of mankind in ancient times. The Druids embraced this knowledge and continued a veneration of the one true God. Using Hebrew science and mathematics, they built amazing stone structures, celebrating the presence of God in nature. They taught their wisdom to the ancient Greeks. Pythagoras himself was a Druid. Naturally, the Druids resisted the barbarous pagan ways of the Romans, but when Christianity came along they recognized it as the natural successor of their own faith, embraced it whole-heartedly and became the founders of the English church, which continued to be far purer than any Christianity that ever came out of Rome. Their legacy remains with us to this day, and there is no inherent discord between Christianity and Druidry.

Druid story number two

The Druids were the dark priests of a dire blood cult that sacrificed beautiful virgins so that the victim's blood would drench the stones of their terrible altars. They were power hungry and controlled the masses by a mixture of tricks, conjuring and terrifying proclamations. With a priesthood of manipulative, lecherous old men, they predated those weaker than themselves, worshipping in dark places and honoring false gods. They liked to burn victims in giant wicker men, and their rites were just an excuse for orgies and killing. Then the much more enlightened presence of the Romans brought civilization to the dark haunts of the Druids. The noble Romans were quick to flush out these practitioners of human sacrifice, and to free their people from slavery and superstition. As the Druids were wiped out, there was much rejoicing.

Druid story number three

While the Druids themselves did not raise the great stone circles of Britain, they were the natural inheritors of the builders. Peaceful, nature worshipers and vegetarians, they were healers and teachers, taking care of their people. They were famed across ancient Europe for their great wisdom and skill, such that those who wished to learn travelled colossal distances to access their wisdom. They were early proponents of sexual equality, holding women in equal respect and having priests of both genders. They celebrated the cycle of the seasons. Suggestions of blood sacrifice were simply the works of Roman propaganda merchants who wished to besmirch them and justify Roman oppression. In reality, the Romans feared the huge political influence Druids had as the counselors of Kings, and feared that Druids would lead uprisings against them. For this reason attempts were made to wipe them out while other local religions were not attacked to the same degree. However, the Druids survived, continuing to pass on their teachings, much of which remains encoded in the work of mediaeval bards and in folklore from Celtic countries. Now that the political and religious climates have changed, those secret societies of Druids have been able to become public again.

Druid story number four

In the beginning, people worshipped the Great Goddess, the Mother Earth. They were ruled by women, and lived in peace. The Druids are just another face of patriarchy as male dominated religions drove out the priestesses and subverted the nature cults, bringing sorrow and disharmony to all lands.

Druid story number five

After the fall of Atlantis, the wise and ancient race that had built the drowned city took refuge in England, where they built Stonehenge and coded their vast wisdom into stories that could be passed down through future generations. They later became the Druids, who are the only true inheritors of the wisdom and mysteries of Atlantis. The ancient Druids/Atlanteans understood electricity and the movement of the stars. They built Stonehenge to be a giant calculator of astronomical events.

Druid story number six

There never were any Druids. Certainly, the Celts had their priests and their intellectuals, like every other people of the time, but there was nothing remarkable about them. Roman writers coined the term 'Druid' and knowing their readers had a taste for lurid details – especially where the activities of distant savages were concerned – they set about writing stories. Thus 'Druids' are no more real than Tolkien's races. We constantly underestimate the literary nature of the classical peoples and their sheer inventiveness. Later stories coming from the Irish are simply the literary creations of the period and as such are due every respect. Those things folklorists have pointed to as remnants of paganism or Druidry even in more recent practice should instead be ascribed to the ingenuity of the rural population that created them. Ours is not the only historical period to produce both fiction writers and pageantry, and we do a disservice to the creativity of our more recent ancestors when we imagine they were re-telling old religious stories rather than inventing something of their own.

The realm of myth

There are no doubt many more such tales to tell, each entirely incompatible with its fellows, difficult to prove, and not entirely possible to disprove. This is the realm of myth.

To what extent does a religion need to have its myths rooted in established fact? Christianity has thus far survived the transition from Bible as literal truth, to Bible as important myth. The facts just don't support it as a literal interpretation of human history, but it's weathered that. A quick glance at any world religion soon makes apparent that hard facts are not required for a belief system to function. Humans are remarkably good at believing in all kinds of things even in face of evidence to the contrary.

Where then should modern pagan faiths position themselves with regard to their own historical origins? Do we need to be ancient in order to be taken seriously? Or to put it another way, even if we could prove that we were authentically re-producing the rituals and beliefs of ancient pagans, do we honestly imagine this would cause us to be taken seriously by those who currently find reasons to mock? That stretches my capacity for belief, certainly.

There is also the issue of our integrity. Nothing attracts

ridicule like a person who claims as hard fact something the majority know to be rubbish; even if the individual is right. To what extent do we trumpet personal truth at the expense of looking foolish? To what extent do we bow to current understandings of ancient history as put forward by historians when that doesn't sit well beside our own myths? Should we cling to the spiritual integrity we find in our own stories, or be led by contemporary research? We live in an age where information is everywhere, but working out the comparative value is difficult. Who is telling the truth? Who has the right story?

Let's go back to the myths for a moment. My mythic ancient Druids (and I think I'm not alone in this perception) were of the wise model. They were the teachers, scientists, philosophers and inventors of their day. If my mythic Druids were real, would they put research first, or myth? As I contemplate this issue, I find it very easy to picture a vigorous debate. Is the old story more important than the latest insight? How does it affect our understanding of the world? What does it mean? Can we work productively with this, or will it limit us? Is it useful? The Druids I imagine would, of course, be the people doing the cutting edge research and the people keeping the old stories, and the people arguing over the significance of both and whether they can usefully be integrated. It is entirely possible that my mythic Druids have been informed by experience of modern Druids and my fantasies, but this is the story I am working with, and what my myth tells me is that I have to consider everything, as best I am able.

At the very least, if I want to go out into the world calling myself a Druid, then how I live has to have some consistency with how I postulate my ancient Druids as being. If I claim them as scientists and historians, I cannot then go on to reject the work of contemporary scientists and historians where it impacts on my understanding of those historical Druids. In imagining my ancestors, I am also inventing myself.

Chapter Three

Spotting the Melons

How do we, as pagan readers, tackle books about historical paganism and separate the good information from the rubbish? Books themselves convey a sense of authority – merely that someone has seen fit to publish them suggests that they are to be taken seriously. Of course many books are self published, and no one has vetted them. This is increasingly tricky to spot, especially if the name of a vanity publisher is given. I've worked at the editorial end of the publishing industry for about a decade. Editors are, on the whole, experts at editing. They are seldom experts in the field of the author's endeavors and may have taken the text on trust, especially if the author appears qualified. However, qualifications and experience in one field do not mean a person can be relied on in another – as the example of Robert Graves has already indicated. Just because the author claims to have a doctorate, and you do not, does not mean you can safely absorb their words as truth.

Where you come to a book knowing more than the author and can spot the factual inaccuracies, evaluating the book is fairly straightforward. The difficulty lies when you are new to a subject. The first few books we read on any topic tend to inform our understanding of it, with all subsequent material read in light of what we already think we know. To avoid being horribly misled by the mistakes and fantasies rife in pagan history, a reader has to be able to assess a book purely in reference to itself, to decide whether the content is reliable.

Below is a list of indicators that a book is not trustworthy. I doubt it's an exhaustive list. Many books will not be guilty of all these failings; in fact the majority will fall into a grey area where you may suspect there is a mix of factually solid information and dubious assertion. It is possible to separate these out from each other, sometimes. All of the textual examples given in this chapter come from 'The Life and Death of a Druid Prince' by Anne Ross Ph. D and Don Robins.[35] It is a text expressing their theory that Celtic bog body, Lindow Man, was an Irish Druid prince offered as a human sacrifice because of the Roman invasion.

Assertion of un-sourced facts: There is a tension, especially in books targeted at a popular market, between narrative and explanations. Explaining uncertainties of interpretation and sources of evidence breaks the flow of the story. However, if all you get is story, you aren't seeing the evidence on which assertions are based and are therefore unable to consider it for yourself to see if you agree with the deductions. As we've already explored, the facts are not always as self evident as story-style history will encourage you to believe. Conversely, where an author explains their reasons for thinking things happened in a certain way and cites their sources, this is a good sign. If some content is sourced and other content merely stated, it may be fair to assume that the assertions are not as well evidenced as the author wishes you to think.

Fact creation: An idea first presented as a theory or possibility transforms, over a few lines or pages, into a fact which is then used to support other theories. For example Lindow Man had apparently eaten burned bread. Starting from the theory that he is a willing sacrifice means this bread is interpreted as being his last, ceremonial, meal and therefore the burned element, it is claimed, means that the bread was part of how he was chosen, or symbolically presented himself, and therefore we are encouraged to deduce that the making of the bread product is itself a ceremonial act, such that by page 39 we can be told that, 'Since the preparation and cooking of the pancake was surrounded by complex rites...' It is the stating of a sacrificial victim theory as an established fact that allows other evidence to be interpreted in ways that support the original theory. This is circular logic and highly suspect. Equally the idea that he might be a Druid morphs into the assertion that he is a Druid. The speculation that he could be Irish becomes an assertion, by page 121 that he 'could only have come from Ireland' despite a total lack of evidence in support of either shift. If we first encounter an idea as speculation, we are more likely to accept it as a possibility, but when authors take that possibility and, without the aid of real evidence, start presenting it as established fact, they deliberately attempt to mislead the reader. It is both cynical and manipulative.

Folklore assumptions: Any book that tries to use folk traditions from the past few hundred years as evidence of what our ancient ancestors did, is highly suspect. It assumes continuity based on no evidence for it. It almost always assumes that ancient pagan practices are there to be uncovered and then duly interprets them into the available information. For example on page 58 the fox fur headband of traditional long sword dancers is seen as directly connected with the fox fur band on Lindow Man's arm. The assumption is that ordinary people doing traditional things are just carrying on, in their ignorant and unimaginative ways, the things they have always done, and that smarter people can come in and understand what it really means. It's a patronizing, outdated and illogical way of assessing the relationship between past and present and tends to indicate that the author knows very little about folk traditions and their origins.

Ignoring the obvious: If a very obvious explanation is ignored in favor of a more dramatic, headline-style interpretation, this is a reason for reading cautiously. For example, Lindow Man's burned bit of bread might suggest something like toast, a stale meal reheated at the start of the day, or a small accident in the baking procedure. Anyone who has ever made bread, or who has made bread using traditional ovens or an open fire, knows that burned bits are almost inevitable. The only thing that burned bread is evidence of, is that he ate some burned bread. Beyond that, all is speculation. Equally, being hit from above does not necessarily mean kneeling to accept a blow. It could mean being attacked when you were already bent over or had been knocked down. It might mean your opponent was on horseback and you were not. If the mundane and normal is overlooked in favor of melodrama, the author may well have been more interested in creating some excitement than in getting the facts straight. Equally the nakedness of Lindow Man is taken by Ross and Robins as further evidence of his status as willing sacrifice, when it would also be consistent with having been killed by someone who wished to steal everything he had of value, which would likely include clothing.

Internal Inconsistency: If a book cannot maintain the coherence of its own arguments, it is probably worthless. An example of this would be, that the whole Ross/Robins argument for Lindow Man being a Druid hinges on this assertion – 'Lindow Man was remarkably unblemished... We wondered how that could be if he had been a veteran warrior', on page forty four. This makes an interesting comparison with this earlier assertion from page twenty nine: 'The fracturing of part of the rear ribcage seemed to have occurred in life.'

Classical and biblical vagueness: References to content from unnamed 'classical authors' or the Bible, or anything of that ilk, where no text is offered, and no context given, are suspect. It is not easy to tell whether the author has read and understood the source in context, or whether they are repeating someone else's assertions, or cherry picking bits that suit them in a distorting way. Using any vague references as evidence or as the basis of authority is highly suspect.

Arbitrary narrowing of options: Most things will have a plethora of potential explanations. There is a method for propping up poor arguments which goes as follows. The author selects two possible explanations, one they want to push through, and one which is obviously farfetched, offering them as the only available interpretations. Rejecting the outrageous one, the author then claims that this lends credibility to the pet theory. Be wary of over simplification, and any suggestion that there are only two or three possible explanations. There are usually a very large number of potential explanations for anything, especially where evidence is sparse.

Spurious associations: By cross referencing to things in other times, places, or cultures the author attempts to establish credibility for their theory. The more distant the cross reference, the more caution must be applied when considering how useful this is. Something close in space, or time may be highly relevant, while superficial similarities with distant things can be misleading. Diversions into barely relevant historical fact can be used to pad both a book and the argument, giving a false impression of scholarship and knowledge. For example, Ross and Robins go to great length to establish that some Celtic noblemen were called Lovernios, a name they associate with foxes and claim for Lindow Man on the basis of his fox fur armband. No amount of evidence for other people having the name establishes that this particular individual was known as Lovernios. No amount of linguistic evidence (which I for one am not equipped to assess the validity of) connecting fox to Lovernios means that a fox fur band equates to having the name. Such associations of information act as window dressing around creative speculation, intended to make it look like a logical argument. The sheer quantity of information involved can make it hard to pick out where the lines of connection are supposed to be and it is easy to assume that they exist and we missed them, when in fact we are being deliberately misled.

This is pagan: If the author asserts that a thing clearly is pagan and moves on to discuss it in those terms, be cautious.

There should be an explanation for the reason it is considered to be pagan, and if that reason comes back to interpreting ancient pagan roots into modern folk practice, the book is highly suspect. An example from page sixty nine: 'The hood game has attracted a veneer of mediaeval legend involving the retrieval of a hood lost by Lady de Mowbray but there is little doubt that the core is pagan.' No justification is offered for this assertion and the activity is then interpreted as the relic of a pagan ceremony, and deductions about its significance are made on the basis of this assumption. If a writer commences by claiming a thing to be pagan and only then can make sense of it as a pagan expression, we should mistrust the conclusions. Only that which speaks for itself as pagan – as a recognized temple site or religious text would – should be considered purely in those terms. There are almost always other available interpretations.

Generalizations: If a book depends on sweeping generalizations to justify its arguments then there are reasons to be suspicious. The broader and less substantiated the assertion, the more caution it requires. Page seventy one gives this example: 'Such beliefs were a vital part of all the agricultural religions.' It is perhaps no accident that the authors have just referenced Frazer and the Golden Bough. Gross generalizations about beliefs and practices across long stretches of time and great swathes of geography are at best going to be too vague to assist. They are also more likely to be wrong. This particular assessment of 'all the agricultural religions' derives from Frazer's work, and depends upon the assumption that all 'primitive' peoples, historical and modern, are much alike, and that clever non-primitive people can read things into their quaint ways. If my writing around this topic sounds subjective and angry, it is because this mindset infuriates me and I am offended by it, especially where it manifests in more recent works whose authors really have no excuse.

Over interpretation: One known fact does not prove great deal. It is dangerous to extrapolate too much from a single detail or observation. Just because a thing happened once does not make it widespread. If that one fact is then taken out of context it can easily be misrepresented to suggest something that is not really fair. The quantity of evidence underpinning an argument needs considering, if that's at all visible. Anything taken to represent more than itself may be misleading.

The unknown game: It is possible to create very neat arguments in any field of study, explaining observations in terms of what is already known and accepted. It is tempting to slot new information into the existing story, assuming firstly that what we thought we knew was right, and secondly that it represents the bigger picture. However, what we do not know often outweighs what we do know. Inevitably we don't have much sense of what we don't know, either. There are two potential traps here – one is to take what is unknown as justification for wild imaginings, and the other is to ignore the possibility that the picture we had before was wrong. Just because a gap exists and a thing could have happened, does not establish that it did. These speculations are easier to spot than the ones that depend on the assumption of already having the gist of it. Just because a piece of information has been aligned with an existing idea does not mean it belongs there, or creates good evidence. The more strident the unexplained assertion that one thing connects to another, the more reason there is to be cautious.

Assumed causality: It is very easy to observe two things and assume a connection, especially if there are reasons of geography or time frame to support this. However, unless a clear, evidenced line of reasoning can be shown, it is unwise to state causality. Ross and Robins assess that Roman activity become more oppressive around the time of Lindow Man's death and that his sacrifice was a consequence of this. He may be a sacrifice, that's speculation. There apparently was the attack on Anglesey and the Iceni rebellion in the right sort of time frame. Does one automatically link to the other? Why should it? There might be a connection, but that does not rule out all the other myriad potential explanations. Looking into the past we only ever see parts of what happened. It is easy to focus on them and assume they make a single coherent picture, but safer not to assume anything at all.

Secret knowledge: If an author claims to have secret knowledge, or secret sources that they refer to but decline to explain, put the book in the recycling. Usually authors are more subtle, and will talk about 'hidden meanings' or 'secret significance'. 'It told us something about his status, something very important, if we could decipher its terse and cryptic message.' This on page fifty two refers to the fox fur armband. Here the authority of the author is established. Only they, with their advanced intellect and great learning, have the skills to unravel the mystery. It is the kind of writing that is designed to inflate the value of the author in the reader's eyes. It also functions to undermine the reader as an intelligent participant in the process, encouraging us to feel like a less clever figure, who can receive wisdom from the great one, but who cannot be expected to figure it out for themselves. It is the life-blood of conspiracy theory writing, and is all chicanery. Anyone with the will and imagination can read any meaning they like into any fact they pick on. It doesn't prove anything. It is unsubstantiated imagination, and where it is accompanied by this kind of attempt to impress the reader into believing, it should be discarded as the worthless rubbish it is.

Could have assertions: Anything could have happened in between what we know about the world. Aliens could have built Atlantis. Druids could have all worn pink. The English Royal family could all be shape shifting lizards. Lindow Man could have been a sacrifice, but he could have been a murder victim, or put to death for a crime. Anyone can speculate, and just because something could have happened, has little bearing on whether or not it did. We are also restricted by our ability to imagine what could have happened, and the more a book focuses on what the author imagines, the more closed it may be to seeing what the evidence suggests. It is very hard to learn anything new when you are obsessed with wrapping your own story around the available information. Most historical writing will include a degree of speculation, but its relationship with the proffered evidence needs considering. Is it the basis of the argument, or a pondering in the conclusion? Does it take the facts and make plausible suggestions, or does it take the gaps and throw ideas at them? The former is entirely legitimate, the latter is of far less use to us.

Judgmental and emotive language: Most historical books are written with an authoritative voice. This style conveys the impression of objectivity, and by its very nature suggests that it is offering hard facts. If that objective voice then gives you the terrible facts, the awful truth, the dreadful revelation, you may inadvertently swallow a value judgment along with the data. A truly neutral, objective voice does not include emotional or judgmental language. It is entirely different to offer a personal interpretation. You may have noticed that where I want to insert my own emotional responses, I shift into a different voice. I use the first person, as here, and I acknowledge the emotional content as being mine, not something inherent to the evidence. If I am horrified, I should put it that way. If I tell you that the evidence is horrific, I am making a value judgment for you that may create a misleading impression of the evidence itself. From page one hundred and twenty four of the dreaded book… 'Let us try and see that bleak and nightmarish picture of a collapsing world…' When a book has this kind of content on every page, the author is more interested in sensationalism and eliciting an emotional reaction than they are in anything else. As a consequence it becomes necessary to treat all such assertions with caution. It is possible to get something useful out of a book that does this, but a careful unpicking of value judgments from facts is called for, and takes time. Better writing will not include such tricks.

Lindow Man stories

Here are a few possible stories about what happened to Lindow Man. Some are more serious and likely than others, all utilize at least something from the available information. One of them may even be right, but that will be a freak accident and in no way intentional on my part. I offer them to illustrate the potential for multiple interpretations.

Story 1

Lindow Man was in a bit of a hurry that morning and burned his toast. He had to bend over to adjust his shoe, having failed to put it on properly in the first place. At this point he was set upon by robbers, who beat him about the head with an axe, stabbed him and then stole everything he had, including his clothes, before throwing him in a pool to hide the evidence of their crime.

Story 2

Lindow Man was a Druid priest who, having been out in the wilds, had not been killed at Mona with the others. However, the Romans were on to him. He was on the run. Breakfast had been a hasty affair, a snatched bit of burned bread. Roman cavalry soldiers hunted him down, the blows from above explained by their being on horseback. They were young and afraid of his curses, which is why they did such an 'overkill'.

Story 3

Lindow Man was a Celtic nobleman who had betrayed his people to the Romans. When justice finally caught up with him, he had enough honor left to kneel for the blow, accepting that he had committed a terrible wrong and should be punished for it.

Story 4

Lindow Man was the victim of such a bizarre accident that his family assumed he must have been cursed. His body was disposed of in the nearby bog as being the only way to ensure that his ill luck was not transferred to his next of kin.

Story 5

Lindow Man's family came from Atlantis. This is why he alone could be the sacrifice. His blood was taken in a rite meant to echo the Christian Eucharist, and all his followers drank it in memory of him.

Speculation tells us very little. It is a way of showing off our ability to make stories and have clever ideas, but it does not open the past to us reliably.

Chapter Four

The Importance of Ancestors

Why does any of this matter? The past is unavailable to us, full of uncertainty, and impossible to visit. What we know will always be vastly outweighed by all that we do not know, and certainty will always be illusive, or illusionary. We are here and now, with the future stretched before us. Is the best answer to all the troubles of our ancestry simply to put it all aside, think no more of it, and move on?

Whether we think about ancestry at a personal level, or in terms of epic sweeps of history, the one thing I think can be said with confidence is that the consequences do not go away just because you ignore them. At an individual level, we are shaped by the families and cultures we grow up in. 'Truths' passed down from previous generations, habits of thought, manners of speech, aspirations, values and modes of behavior come to us from our ancestry whether we like it or not.

> *Opening these books, one is arrested with a pang as if the dead got up and spoke forcibly, freshly from the page… If there is a sense that we are all informed by the whole of the past (even those parts which seemed to flake away into oblivion) then these women… being our past, are also part of us.*[36]

I am a firm believer in the ability of people to choose. I do not think that our DNA or the effects of our ancestral lineage, shape us beyond our control. They give us the raw material we start with. All that we inherit serves to predispose us in certain ways, but we are not fated to repeat the sins of our fathers, or grand-mothers, or great, great, great ancestors whose stories are lost but whose influence remains in our blood. Nor does a grand and heroic ancestry guarantee that we too will be remarkable and worthwhile people. We have plenty of opportunities to fall and fail by our own efforts. We can choose to replicate behaviors, or to reject them, but it's easier to do that if you are conscious of what you have inherited. While the gifts of our ancestors represent an unchallenged vision of normality, we cannot break with the past easily, or hope to become separate from all that has been bequeathed to us.

It takes awareness to break chains of all kinds. Chains of victimhood and abuse. Chains of poverty and desperation. Chains of hopelessness. And, at a collective level, we can think of all the other things our wider ancestry has given us – all that we have inherited and taken onboard as the normal way of the world. None of the things around us are inevitable or eternal. Anything can be changed in terms of human culture and action, if sufficient will is brought to bear. The more we understand how we got here, the better able we are to pick our own way forward rather than being herded along blindly by the still-influencing actions of those who came before us.

Ancestry shapes not only individual identity, but also the forms of races, nations and religions that influence us. We define ourselves in relation to so many things, the vast majority of which have a history and direction of their own. So much of race, nation and religion is also myth. It is the exporting of ideals and hopes into the past to validate the present. The appropriation of history for control and manipulation is widespread. Look at how any right wing organization plays with fantasy ideas about racial purity to stir up aggression against 'outsiders'. Consider how the age of an institution is used to validate it. 'Tradition' and 'heritage' are words used to justify all kinds of acts, including animal cruelty, genital mutilation and discrimination. Just because we've been doing something for a long time does not make it a good thing. After all, as a species we've probably spent more time assuming the earth to be flat than we have thinking it to be round. We've spent more time in tyrannies than democracies, and slavery has a very long tradition. Using the age of a thing to justify its existence is a poor argument indeed.

We use history and ancestry to justify and validate ourselves. It gives us a context. We do this because it is what our people have always done. We might claim that we can't help doing it for all manner of reasons: We grew up with it. It's part of our culture. Where we come from, it's normal. Fine. Expected. We are not responsible. Is this really how we want to be?

It's easy to hide behind our ancestors. Not least because most of them are dead and get no say in our uses and misuse of them. Every time we ascribe something to our heritage, we disempower ourselves.

Let me create an imaginary story for you, that I have an anxious disposition. This is not my fault because my mother was very anxious and suffered from many phobias, I grew up learning to be afraid of everything. But this was not her fault either because her mother was very anxious although back then no one really diagnosed it, and her grandfather suffered shell shock during the First World War, so perhaps it all stems back to him. This is a story. It happens not to be true, but even if the facts were accurate, it would still be a story. Its function is to give me no power at all over my own mental health, and to make it hard for me to seek help. Anxiety in this story is 'normal' for my family, so I do not need to take responsibility for it or attempt to tackle it. This gives me the perfect excuse to relinquish control over my life. I could tell the same story in terms of abuse, or anger. I could talk about depression in the same way, or obsessive compulsive behavior. The effects would be the same – to create a story that makes it impossible to change anything.

Why would I do this? Change is frightening. Having things stay the same is reassuring and familiar, even if it is unpleasant. 'Better the devil you know' is one of those nasty little memes that contributes to keeping people locked into destructive, life-sapping situations. Most of us fear change, to some degree. Many of us fear responsibility. If the problem lies outside us, we do not have to shoulder the burden of fixing it. This is easier, and apparently more comfortable, but every time we give away ownership of our lives in this fashion, we give away freedom and happiness as well. We give up another chance to lead more fulfilling and enjoyable lives. Perhaps on some level we imagine we deserve it. Our ancestors had no better, why should we ask for more?

If we look to our ancestors for security and a sense of place in the world, then anything that rejects them, also casts us adrift. It's one of the hardest things for students from poor backgrounds who are clever – going to university represents a change of culture that will to some degree alienate you from your family. Your life will be vastly different to theirs. You will never be the same as young folk who come from rich and educated backgrounds, but you no longer fit in where you came from either. The desire not to reject our families often keeps us where we arrived, repeating what went before us.

The desire to belong is natural, essential even. The need to be part of a group and have a place in the world is vital for emotional wellbeing. We are not meant to exist in isolation. And yet to live our own lives and be our own people, we must to some extent move away from the nest, the old values, the previous ways of understanding things. How far do we have to go? How much should we give up, and how much should we hang on to?

There are no tidy answers to such questions – inevitably this is all individual and will depend to a degree on where we came from and where we long to be. Finding our place as distinct individuals whilst holding relationship with family, society, culture and ancestry, is not easy. Especially not if you are drawn to something very different from everything you know your predecessors have done.

If we like the world just the way it is, then there is no reason to leave the nest or seek new ways. People who are drawn to paganism and Druidry have usually already rejected something from their immediate ancestry – and often more than just religious beliefs. Paganism is radically green spirituality. To claim kinship with nature is to align yourself in opposition to the driving forces in modern culture – consumerism and greed. To be a Druid is to reject so much of what our recent ancestors of place and blood have bequeathed to us. It is to reject systems and priorities, and seek after something else. Yet, at the same time, Druidry calls for an honoring of the ancestors, and it calls for peace within us. How do we reconcile such conflicting impulses? How do we make peace with our ancestors – immediate and distant – whilst rejecting all the ideas and assumptions that have brought our culture to its current state?

With difficulty, is going to be the short answer. The longer answer involves time, patience, and compassion. It is possible to reject an idea, or behavior, without rejecting a whole person or an entire way of life. We have to pick carefully through the grey areas, seeking out that which inspires, rejecting that which no longer works. It is an inevitably subjective process, full of opportunities for self-indulgence and misplaced justifications. Equally it is a process with the potential to inform and inspire.

While there are negative aspects to ancestry to contend with, there is also much good to be found in tapping into the past. I am increasingly convinced that our sense of geographical place can be hugely influenced by a sense of ancestral belonging. When our ancestors of blood belong to the landscape we occupy, this can create a powerful feeling of relationship and belonging. Talking to people with broken lineage, the issue of belonging to a place may be as important for some as belonging to a bloodline, and the two can run very close together.

As we journey into the stories of our ancestors, so we also journey into stories of ourselves, unpicking the myths we have made about our identities and perhaps creating new, more functional stories that help us move forwards.

We also journey into the shared ancestry of modern Druids, with all its myths, uncertainties and problems. We cannot create a modern Druid way by ignoring history, or fabricating it further, but honest relationship with what is known presents all kinds of challenges that we need to face as a community. In this too, we need to rethink our stories, and re-write our myths.

The journeys we each make as individuals are part of the complex journey through time our communities are making, our nations, even our species. Recorded history may focus on big names and dates, but those are the culmination of lives lived, choices made, and the actions of countless unnoticed individuals.

In this context of interconnectedness, it often makes sense to me to speak of ancestry in broad strokes, looking back at the ancient past, and the more recent, alongside speaking in much more intimate and personal terms. We all had ancestors alive at any time in history we care to contemplate. Our existence is due to the day-to-day life-and-death decisions they made, to the normal, small accidents and coincidences that each existence depends on. All of history is our ancestry, and I think we ought to take that personally. It is fundamental to our shared humanity, and our equality of worth. The wondrous improbability that any of us came to be born, that so many lives and deaths fell into place in just the right way to result in us, is a universal miracle that none of us should underestimate. In honoring our ancestors, we celebrate the flow of life energy, one generation to the next, which brought us into being.

There probably wasn't anything deliberate in the enormity of ancestral couplings that led to any of us specifically being here. There has been no grand plan since the dawn of time, destined to result in any one of us specifically. And yet, here we all are. Whether or not we beget offspring of our own, we are all links in the ancestral chains connecting past to future. We none of us ever fully know what impact our lives have, or what might have been different had we never lived. We each contribute to the world events of our time, largely unable to discern our own impact. And yet it must exist, just as each water droplet contributes to the ocean. We are special beyond measure. And so is everyone else.

The ancestors teach us about both the tenacity and fragility of life. Working with them invites us to look at ourselves anew, and with wonder. It gives reason to appreciate life as a precious, sacred force and to respect it. Each life is unique. Each one of us is a creation crafted from the entire history of a planet. I think we could afford to take that a lot more seriously than we do.

Chapter Five

Fantasy Ancestors

Fantasy ancestors might or might not be real but they can have colossal influence on us. Their function in our lives is not to be an accurate representation of what was, but to give us a place to stand. In some ways, this can be tremendously powerful, especially for people who are in some way disenfranchised. It can also be emotionally and intellectually fraudulent. As soon as we step away from our known and immediate ancestry and into the realms of speculation, we move closer to our fantasy ancestors. To a large extent we cannot reconstruct any meaningful sense of the past without peopling it with individuals, and as we have so little solid information to guide us, the further back we go, the more gaps we have to fill in, until story far outweighs accepted fact.

Humanizing the past in a way that makes it comprehensible is absolutely necessary if history is to have any emotional resonance for us. An ancestry of faceless, unfeeling people is impossible to engage with. Without empathy, without imagining ourselves in their shoes, the past would be a series of technical details. We need that imaginary engagement to bring it to life in ways we can understand. This is why we keep turning history into books and films. We want it to make sense, and we want to make it relevant to us. We normally assume that the essence of human emotion hasn't changed much over time, and we also assume that the emotions and motivations of our ancestors are comprehensible to us. We could be very wrong in this, but so be it. We can only work within the confines of our own understanding.

We have been writing fictionalized histories for about as long as people have been writing anything at all down, by the looks of things. As far as I know, creation myths exist in all religions, and I've yet to hear tell of any tribe, or culture that does not have some kind of story about where it came from and who it is. Stories have a way of growing all by themselves when they are retold. The good bits get embellished, the dull bits drop out with retelling. Tales become larger, bolder, more dramatic, heroic, romantic and engaging. Where people are literate, story-making, and reliant on oral traditions for their history, the lines between truth and myth are always going to be blurry. Those involved in the story-making will not necessarily know if they are telling an unadorned truth. However, there is a border to cross into an entirely different country, where all semblance of fact parts company from the tale. It's a hard border to find and an easy one to inadvertently cross.

It's easy to say that making up pretend ancestors who make us seem important is dishonest, self deluding, dishonorable and generally to be discouraged. If the fraud is believed, it can cause all kinds of difficulty and harm. If the fantasy is detected, the fraudster looks like a fool, at best. There have always been people who have claimed blood ties to those with power and wealth, have claimed to descend from figures of cultural importance, or from secret magical societies. Usually it's hard to prove anything one way or the other. Deliberate fraud for financial and social gain is easily skipped over as an issue because there's not much to debate there, it is simply dishonorable. However, this is not the only way in which we create fantasy ancestors. Many of them are not necessarily bad for us, or unethical.

The changelings

There's an old folk theme that manifests in lots of different stories, about how faeries would steal human children and leave a faerie in its place, to be raised like a cuckoo by the unwitting parents. If you don't believe in faeries, the logical explanation is that the tale was created to explain disabled or troubled children in the days before we had any understanding of autism, learning disabilities or the causes of many physical ailments.

It is also a story that can be used to explain being a fey child in an ordinary family. In many ways, Harry Potter taps straight into this myth – the wizard child in the muggle household, he too is an archetype for everyone who grew up in a place they clearly didn't fit. Most changeling children are not reclaimed by the faeries, nor are they whisked away to magical school and the life they secretly knew should have been theirs all along. Most grow up, and struggle along with the world as best they can. A significant number find their way into paganism and a sense of home and family that has been missing until then.

The changeling child does not belong. In order to survive, they may have to learn how to fake fitting in. Also, in order to survive, they may carry with them an untold story of the place where they do belong. Fairy tales old and new are full of frogs who turn out to be princes, ugly ducklings who turn out to be swans after all, abandoned children who turn out to be long lost and treasured descendants of great families, misfits who are really witches, fairies, werewolves, Jedi knights. There are so many stories about the child who turns out to belong somewhere else after all, and so few people who will actually admit to carrying such a story. Perhaps we all did, and no one mentions it. Were we all secret princesses, misplaced swans and changeling children?

My own awareness of not fitting came on slowly, and was more about not fitting into the mainstream. It wasn't until the birth of my own child that I found my changeling story. My son arrived with pointed ears, like a little elf. When my grandmother saw him for the first time, she said, 'He's got Hunking ears. Like you did. It's the Cornish pisky blood.'

Of course I didn't fit. I am an elf, from a long line of elves. Cornish elves no less, for added authenticity. I even have an acute iron and steel allergy to back it up. I tell the story sometimes, light-heartedly. If anyone imagined I was serious about the being-an-elf thing, they would also consider me mad. But in the secret places in my head, the bits no sane person ever shares with the world, of course I know I'm an elf, and that my ancestors were Cornish piskies, because that would explain everything. It feels weird writing this here, but I've learned over the years with teaching that being vague, general and talking about 'other people' doesn't work. If I am to share anything meaningful, a little soul-baring is required. Sometimes a lot. If I say it first, other people have the space to say it too. My fantasy ancestors are elves.

If I'd gone out into the world and claimed this gave me special authority to teach authentic Cornish pisky magic on very expensive courses, that would be one thing. But this is just between me, and my family, and part of how I cope with feeling perpetually at odds with the world. I'm able to hold it in a strange, story place where it is both taken seriously by me, and not taken seriously by me. In other words, I know this is a myth I carry about myself, and like all myths, it might, or might not have some truth in it. The steel and iron allergies at least, are entirely real, and I do have Cornish ancestors.

I've met two women who are mermaids, and although I don't think they knew each other, they are curiously alike. Their eyes are uncannily similar, and both have long, reddish, mermaid hair and always seem to be somewhere else. Both confessed to a fascination with mermaids. Neither claimed to be mermaids in any literal sense, but the Cornish pisky in me took one look at them both and knew perfectly well that in their hearts, they carried that story about themselves. They were mermaids, lost to the sea.

There are traditional stories of shape shifters who lose their other skins and are trapped in human form. The selkie is a figure of not belonging. They may also be a convenient explanation for how you mysteriously fell pregnant when you shouldn't have done! Even modern fairy tales like Pirates of the Caribbean do this, with a goddess trapped in human form. It's implicit in most of the superhero stories, the waking one day to amazing powers and the scope to change the world. It is both aspiration, and a reflection of some inner part we just know isn't like the rest of the world at all.

Out of these hidden places, we craft some of our fantasy ancestors. These are the faeries who swapped us for the regular child our human parents were expecting. Even if we don't give them names and faces, we carry the sense of them, and the idea that we could belong somewhere else. It gives us an explanation for why we don't fit. That constructing of fantasy ancestors can be a wild, creative process, bringing a much-needed sense of belonging and tribe. Then, if we find others who belong to the same secret tribe, we can perhaps admit it to them.

My witchy granny

She's an almost obligatory icon for pagans. If not literally a granny, then some aged, female relative, or at a pinch, a strange old uncle. The witchy granny is proof that you are a bit special too. She was secretly a pagan back before anyone had heard of Gerald Gardner. She made spells in her kitchen and dished out wisdom. I've been in so many conversations with pagan folk who turn out to have one. Maybe it's the case that a leaning towards paganism does somehow run in families. Maybe we look back at our family stories and interpret them based on need. Maybe we make them up, because we need them to have existed. Everyone should have a witchy granny.

Sometimes the witchy granny is a blatant device, meant to attract kudos and get a person taken seriously. More often she's like a badge of belonging. 'See, I am part of this tribe, I have a granny too.'

My gran was a self-professed Christian and very into Jesus as someone who set an example of how we should all live. She could also look at a person's handwriting and describe them – including things like dress style and hobbies. She had premonitions, and it was her deep love of the natural world that informed some of the key moments in my developing pagan awareness, back when I was a teen. Looking back, I think she was something like a Christian pantheist, but she was also a bit... witchy.

The really interesting figure is her mother, who declined to go to church on the grounds that it made her claustrophobic, and according to family myth, had visions, not just premonitions. I never knew her, she died long before I was born. My gran idolized her, my mother considered her old fashioned and a bit of a curmudgeon. Her presence continued to resonate in my family for decades, and I had for many years what I thought was a very keen sense of her. I won't ever know if there was any accuracy in my perceptions. I often wonder what she would have made of my life.

When I first started getting involved with the pagan scene, I talked about my 'female lineage'. I was very young, entirely untrained, somewhat self-taught, and desperate to be taken seriously. I really do have a female lineage of strange women. It's easy to imagine, considering my mother, grandmother and great grandmother, that it must go further back than that. I clearly come from a long line of witchy women. I belong. I'll say in my defense that I didn't try to make very much capital out of this in my early days, I didn't expect anyone to take me seriously based purely on this, I have always sought to be judged on my actions, but it made me feel more secure as I waded out into some unfamiliar waters. I have a witchy granny too.

One of the good things about the witchy granny archetype is its part in reclaiming feminine knowledge and traditions. The stories, mysteries, skills and trials of our ancestors are still relevant to us, and reclaiming and revaluing female knowledge is important work. Too often the female traditions are written off briefly in one hideous word: housewife. The witchy granny is not a housewife. Her kitchen is a place of magic. Her crafts are many and arcane. What she does, matters. Maybe some of the women we reclaim as witches would have self-identified that way if they'd lived in more liberal times. Maybe not. They might be horrified with how we re-interpret them. I like to think they'd understand, and smile in secret, knowing ways over the funny things we younger generations do, and this too is part of my fantasy ancestry.

My ancient pagan ancestors

Of course we don't know a vast amount about what our pagan ancestors did. I'm going to explore ancestors of tradition in more detail later in the book, but for now I want to raise them purely in their fantasy aspect. These are our ancient ancestors, lost in the mists of time. You can't be a modern pagan for long without managing to form some kind of opinion of your pagan ancestors. Of course as there are different cultures and times to contemplate, it doesn't have to be one all-embracing opinion. There are Druids who see the Romans as on the whole being a decent enough lot with plenty of good ideas, and the Romano-British as being very much where their Druidry has its roots. Others see Romans as evil imperialists who wiped out the Druids and who represent the worst kind of cultural tyranny. Some of us are confident about ignoring claims that the Celts undertook human sacrifice, whilst being equally confident that the Phoenicians did. Others think the Phoenicians were misrepresented. On it goes.

We look back at our pagan ancestors and see something we value. It differs as to what period and geographical area we turn to for inspiration, but something in that pre-Christian thinking calls to us. It might be the idea of less structured religion, despite all the evidence that plenty of pre-Christian cultures were entirely structured about their religions as well. It might be the feeling that our ancestors were closer to nature, understood it and were able to live in far more sustainable ways.

Whatever our personal beliefs, we tend to have a notion of ancestry that supports it. That's a basic sanity issue, as we try to assemble and hold world views that make sense. But it is important to recognize that we may become more interested in holding a story that makes sense in the context of our own lives, than in poking the available information too hard. Ronald Hutton in Blood and Mistletoe makes it clear that there is no straightforward and reliable evidence for anything at all pertaining to the Druids. There is no clear history for us to trust. Does this cause me, or any other modern Druid necessarily, to relinquish a belief that there were historical Druids? Probably not. Does the absence of hard evidence in any way undermine my perception of ancient Druids? As far as I can tell, my myths are all intact. Clear evidence would have been a different matter, and I would, I assume, have done my best to integrate that into the stories I have. If needs be, the stories would have had a serious overhaul, but I wouldn't have given them up. Like most modern Druids, I reject the bits of Roman writing I don't like and embrace the bits I find relevant. That is not the work of a diligent academic, but the inclinations of a storyteller, a mythmaker.

This too, is not new. It is simply a thing that people do. 'Whether anthropological, theological or indigenous folk belief, each generation brings a new personality and point of view to its perception of reality. Thus, the past is always being reviewed and reinvented by insiders as well as outsiders.'[37]

The dark side of fantasy

As mentioned before, fantasy ancestors can be deliberately constructed to give us kudos and authenticity. Such efforts are likely to be the work of clever people who know full well what they are doing and will not be confused by their own creations. However, when the creation of fantasy ancestors is all about self-delusion, the person creating them can genuinely believe their own tales, and be harmed by them. Anything that takes us too far from consensus reality or makes it difficult for us to engage with everyone else, is dysfunctional. It is one thing to take comfort from an idea of fantasy ancestry, and another to go round asserting it in a way that disengages you. Again, there are some very fine lines here, much of which comes down to how we understand our own stories and what we use them for.

I once met a man who had a very complex understanding of ancestry. He felt that there were a set of people within the human gene pool who carried genetic material from some other, older race, which had been integrated with regular humans. Genuine science around the issues of Homo-Sapiens breeding with Neanderthals and other groups fuelled his beliefs that he belonged to this special subset. Unfortunately for me, this subset had obviously elfish traits – the high cheekbones, light bone structures, and fey dispositions. So far this is not a line of thought a million miles from my own fantasy ancestors, which is no doubt why I got to hear so much about it. However, my fantasy ancestors have mostly been there as a sort of comfort-blanket-come-explanation. I don't wave them around because I'm not generally trying to prove anything. The man in this story felt that he belonged to a superior group of people, far more important and worthy than the 'herd' around him. His elfish ancestors justified his feelings of superiority, reinforced racist (speciesist?) ideas, and created a focus for his other antisocial beliefs and activities.

Fantasy ancestors, racism and eugenics can all run together very easily. Racial purity is a nonsense idea, rooted in desires to prove entitlement rather than any kind of reality. In just the same way that some people have tried to prove men are inherently cleverer than women, or that people of African origin are of lower intelligence. It's the kind of appalling 'science' that depends on selective use of evidence, and a great deal of creativity when it comes to interpretation.

We can imagine ancestors to help build a sense of shared

history and through it, community, or we can use it to establish 'us' and 'them'. We can use imagined ancestors to affirm self when life has not given us the blood ancestors we needed, or we can use it to justify and vindicate. Looking at your own beliefs to ascertain whether they exist for beneficial or malevolent reasons is not easy. Anyone determined to delude themselves will not readily be able to relinquish their own illusions. However, that doesn't let any of us off the hook from properly considering how we construct and relate to our ancestors, how we use them, and whether we are acting appropriately and well in relation to them.

In the next sections of the book I'm going to explore in detail the three groups of ancestors identified by modern Druidry. I want to explore how we construct them, where we find them, how we work with them, what potential role they have in our lives, and how we walk those curious lines between myth and reality.

We need myths. We need our myths to be robust and inspiring, helping us make sense of our own lives. Flimsy, self-indulgent myths that pay no regard to reality are of little use. If we accept that solid, dependable historical information is not available to us and that myths are all we get, let us at least craft good and worthy ones that we can be proud of. Let us make the stories of ourselves and our people that will carry us forward, without the shame of being called fraudulent, or insane. Personal stories and stories of the tribe – although often they are the same – can be made today just as they have been historically.

Myth is not an enemy of history, reason or science. It is not a rejection of rationality, or a retreat into the realms of pure fantasy escapism. Good myths are true at an essential level even if the details are extravagant. They tell us who we are and show us where we might be going. They are the stories we make out of reality. The better we understand the real things, the better able we are to craft the soul stories that can bind us in relationship with each other and the wider world.

Chapter Six

Ancestors of Blood

The ancestors of blood are those people from whom we are descended. This makes them the most personal and immediate set of ancestors, some of whom we are likely to be conscious of and influenced by. We have little control over them and unless you believe that you planned this life in some pre-life scenario, we probably didn't choose them. As previously mentioned, if we consider the history of life on earth, we can see our blood ancestry as connecting us to the most ancient and basic forms of existence, and through that, giving us universal relationship with all other life forms. Ancestry thought about on these terms is broad, vague, and only challenges us if we believe our own blood line to be particularly special. In this chapter we'll be exploring the full spectrum of blood ancestry, from the immediate to the ancient.

Personal history

So many pagans come to this spiritual path from other backgrounds. A significant number have rejected the faith of their childhood along the way. That faith belongs to their parents, and probably further back as well. Within families this can cause pain and tension. The rejection of faith is so easily interpreted as a rejection of the parents themselves – and sometimes it is. People are easy to frighten and threaten, and for devoted Christians, a pagan child can be an alarming thing. Fears of evil occultism, Satanism, sexual exploitation and all the horrors of B-movie magic rooted in both popular culture and traditional assumptions about pagans, all come into play. To come out as pagan in a non-pagan family is to take on all the stories the rest of society has about what paganism is and does. Of course for many it's fine, but you never really know until you take the plunge.

Those who reject the religion of their parents are also rejecting the authority of their parents. Most of us, to some degree, go through that process in our teens anyway, it being a necessary part of growing up. To see ourselves as adults, we must necessarily reject any further attempts by other adults to control our lives. We have to take full responsibility for ourselves, but this too is often met with resistance. Families are messy, complex and emotionally challenging, and no one gets out of childhood without a few bumps and scrapes to knees and psyches alike.

I've come to the conclusion that the failure of our parents is inevitable, and our failure as parents (if we go there) equally so. There is no such thing as perfect parenting. Either we are stifled with too much care, or we are not sufficiently watched over. We are given too many boundaries, or not enough. As we climb out of the nest and move away from parental care, we find the ways in which we have not been equipped for the world, or the neurosis we have swallowed whole from our families. We want things our parents do not approve of, or cannot understand. And then we grow up to repeat the whole process with our own offspring.

For most of us, the anger and resentment inherent in being a teenager passes. Our hormones settle down, we find our own place in the world, re-negotiate our familial relationships and get on with life. Not everyone manages this. Not everyone should. I've known guys in their fifties who were still afraid of their mother's wrath. Adults so angry with their family that they can't hold relationship. Adults whose life choices have pushed them out of the family circle, or who just lie by omission so that the family never knows who they are the rest of the time.

The family is, for most of us, the first community we belong to. It's the one that gives us our ideas of 'normal' that inform how we make our way through life. Some of us carry those values wholesale, others go through the painful process of rejecting them. We all want a place to belong, and that first community, that circle of family is the first opportunity we have to achieve that belonging. For those who are rejected, unable to fit, who feel they are never good enough or perceive something in themselves that means their family cannot love them, there is a loss of stability and confidence that comes from this experience. Where the bonds have been broken for us, there can be all kinds of other challenges too.

It isn't necessarily the case that our families deliberately load us up with things that will subsequently drive us mad. As children we hear and understand the world in our own ways. Chance remarks and small misunderstandings can create ideas in us before we are ever properly conscious of them, and we interpret everything else through the filters of those first setbacks.

Very early on in my life, I took on board the idea that I was desperately, hideously, fat. I was a bit rounded as a child – my gran called it puppy fat. Looking back at old photos, I seem fairly normal, but as a child I was agonizingly self-conscious about my weight and shape. I couldn't bear to be looked at. I carried that into my teens. In retrospect, I have no idea how I managed not to become anorexic during my teenage years. It wasn't for lack of trying. I came to equate thinness with loveableness. If I was thin enough, I would be loved. What I didn't understand at the time was that my parent's relationship was breaking down and they were more involved with that, than with me. I look back and wonder if very young inferences about my brother being an unhealthy child, created the association in the first place. He was very thin as a baby, and needed a lot of care, which resulted in me being sent off to granny. This is just speculation, I do not remember a specific moment of deciding that if I could only be thin enough, my family would be as interested in me as they seemed to be in my sibling. Perhaps it was something else entirely.

'Thin' was an easy idea to get my head round. Thin enough would get me a boyfriend, or at least some attention. I starved myself, but I have inherited a tough body (thank you ancestors!) and rather than become the bone-thin waif I longed to be, I adapted and stored. The result was that I became fatter, rather than thinner. Now in my thirties, I am unexpectedly and inexplicably thinner than I have ever been, and finally conscious that, in the dark places inside my head, there was never such a thing as 'thin enough'.

My grandmother, who had gone through the Second World War and rationing, saw food as an expression of love. My mother grew up with that and to some degree rejected it. My maternal great grandmother was the sort to do Sunday high tea with a table cloth, no matter what. My paternal grandmother was in service. Perhaps that's why she liked to put food on the table and disappear into the kitchen while others ate it. I can point in a whole host of directions, in my immediate ancestry, to explain my own poor relationship with food. There was a time when I felt inclined to blame my immediate ancestors for what I had felt compelled to try to do to my body during my teens. I made the choices, not them. I can make other choices, I can decide to accept myself.

Anger and blame don't fix much, and they most certainly do not allow for healing. Whatever issues we have with our most immediate ancestors – as so many of us do – we can only get past that by making peace with ourselves first. Perhaps they are not deliberately doing something to us. Perhaps they are repeating the patterns of their own birth families. The men who cannot express emotion. The mothers who do not know how to hug. The grandparents so afraid we will get ideas above our station that they have to keep knocking us back, for our own protection. The folk who were beaten as children and are sure that's what made them as strong as they are today. The ones who know that if they don't control us, we will make all the mistakes they did.

All children arrive powerless and wholly dependent. They set about growing at a pace it is difficult to keep up with, bodies and minds adapting far faster than our fixed adult forms ever will again. Everything they do is designed to help them not need adults anymore. Watching them pull away, overtake, and rush headlong towards disaster is not an easy process. Sometimes it's in having children of our own that we start to make sense of what our own parents did and why, even if we are keen not to repeat any of it. Many people choose not to have children. There are a great many reasons for making such a choice, and for a lot of deliberately childless folk, this is a positive decision that does not need justifying. However, there are some for whom that choice comes from fearing that they will replicate the behavior of their own parents. Even those with children already, who then become aware of problems in their own background, can then become anxious about parenting. Heritable diseases can also be a painful contributor to this process. For whatever reason it is taken, childlessness should always be a valid and unchallenged choice. However, if a person feels restricted by fear or pain, that needs tackling. That could equally be fear of social ostracism for not reproducing.

Being at peace with our most immediate ancestors requires being at peace with ourselves. It can take considerable picking over of memories and feelings to reach that point. We might not need the archetypal therapist's couch and the invitation to tell someone else about our parents, but to understand ourselves, we do need to explore how we exist in the context of that parental relationship.

When we are children, there is a time when we believe our parents are second only to god. They know everything. They do everything for us. They have the power to permit and refuse, to praise or reject. Our lives depend on their good will and revolve around their ideas about us. We are shaped by them and by the environments they create and expose us to. Our parents are working based on their own experience of being parented and what they have seen elsewhere, with their own tweaks and innovations in the mix as well. As a parent you base your understanding of the child on your memories of being a child. But this new child is not you, and there are no guarantees that they will think or feel in any way you can recognize.

Part of the process of growing up involves the recognition that our parents are not omniscient or omnipotent. Those first encounters with their limitations can be traumatic. The stable certainty we had, believing them second only to god, evaporates. They can make mistakes, act unfairly, do the wrong thing and we are stuck with that. In our teens we may decide that we can, and will be better than our parents. From the parental side it's a hard process too. Some people do genuinely believe in their own infallibility, but most have a more realistic perspective. Not being good enough for your child is fearful, and painful. It is one of the hardest things to admit.

We live in a time when authority is not the be all and end all. Our more immediate ancestors grew up in more structured societies, more overtly patriarchal, where power begat respect, money represented power and you were expected to know your place. Children no longer call their father 'Sir'. I think it makes parenting a lot easier, that we do not have to represent absolute authority to our offspring. The media and politicians decry the loss of respect for official authority alongside this. But respect should be earned through actions, not assumed based on wealth and status. The state is no longer the uber-parent, and we do not feel obliged to honor and humor our mothers and fathers in ways that our ancestors might have done. The old patterns have been eroded, but nothing new and clear has settled to take its place, and we still have to negotiate the power structures of our own families and relationships.

I spoke before of changeling children and people who have grown up with a keen sense of not belonging. I think most of us at some time have wondered if we were adopted, or swapped by mistake in the hospital. For a subset of people, deliberate abuse will have been part of the issue. Child abuse was something even our most recent ancestors did not speak about. The recognition of it is new and the space for children to speak out against adult abusers recent. It is still not easy for a mistreated child to make themselves heard, especially when that mistreatment has been at a parent's hands. Children are most likely to suffer abuse from step parents and step siblings, I gather, but I wonder if the statistics are biased by a willingness to hear some kinds of claim and a reluctance to hear others.

My grandmother was abused by a music teacher. To the best of my knowledge, there was no police involvement. When her parents became aware of the situation, she was kept away from the man. There was no counseling and she suffered for the rest of her life with the legacy of that abuse. How many of our ancestors have such hidden stories? Go back a generation or two and most people didn't believe you could have rape in marriage. The law has been slow to recognize it. Marriage meant you had consented to have sex. How many unspoken wounds lie in our immediate ancestry? And how have they manifested? What unseen things are we still influenced by?

There is no excuse for abusive parenting. Often though, it helps if we have some explanation. A story that makes sense of what was done, and enables us to recognize it as not our fault or our failing. Like sexual abuse issues, mental health problems were swept under the carpet until very recently. Sick and troubled people had no access to support or sympathy, just the pressure to put on a good face, be a man about it, not make a fuss and so forth. When mental illness was widely perceived as weakness, laziness or a direct consequence of vice, who could admit to it? And so the consequences of anguish and shame seep into our lives, unexplained, but having knock-on effects that can travel down through generations. Alcoholism and other addictions are still not easily discussed and may lie in the family's shared skeleton closet. Violence in the home has been, and still is, widespread. It used to be entirely accepted that women and children could be beaten by men and only recently have the police started to intervene in 'domestic' incidents. Its widespread nature did not enable anyone to speak about it, or seek help. Loyalty to the family has long been upheld as a value, divorce was not widely available to our ancestors, and the legacy of historical abuse can remain, haunting younger generations in the form of dysfunctional relationships that are never explained.

I had a pagan friend some years ago whose parents were Christian, and whose family had been bullying her for years. She felt under dreadful emotional pressure from them, and found it difficult to make her own feelings and needs known. She was a beautiful person, a full-figured mother with a generous heart, and pretty by anyone's standards. However, she carried a great deal of pain from her family relationships, not least because, she one day confessed, her mother bullied her continually about being overweight. Her body image and self-confidence had clearly been damaged by this.

Eventually, I met the mother. She was tiny, and bone thin. The lines in her face suggested someone who did not smile much and worried a great deal. She was neat and precise, and every detail of the way she moved and sat suggested total lack of ease with herself. What demons were there gnawing away inside her head? Perhaps like me, she had acquired a belief that thinness and love are the same thing and felt the need to make her daughter understand. When the daughter spoke of her, she seemed a frightening, authoritarian figure, but the woman I met was small in every way. No doubt her private face was different from her public one, but the deep unhappiness in her must have come from somewhere.

Explanations help us make sense of where we are. It is easy to go from there to blame. We can indeed blame people for the things they have done to us, and when relationships are abusive, there is every reason to blame people for their own dreadful actions. However, what we must avoid doing is blaming people for our subsequent behavior, because this is the means by which we perpetuate the problem rather than ending it. If we recognize the faulty thinking handed down from our parents and grand-parents, we can change it. If we use it as an excuse for carrying on in the same way, or for other shortcomings, we pass that historical mess down to the next generation instead.

I once knew a man who had been raised by a feminist mother. According to his accounts, she was at the extreme and man-bashing end of feminism, and brought him up to understand that all men were potential rapists, that men are the cause of all wars, and that as a man he had to learn to control the dangerous potential for brutality within him. His response to this was to cross dress, taking on the authority he associated with his mother by stealing her clothes, and later the clothes of other women. He also went on to rape, whilst holding his mother entirely responsible for his own atrocious behavior.

Our ancestors are not there to be our scapegoats. It does not matter what they show us or do to us, unless we have spent our entire lives locked in their homes and unable to access any other sources of information, we have the scope to learn. We are not required to repeat their mistakes. It is not inevitable that our lives will follow the same pattern as theirs. If we acknowledge the experiences that have shaped us, we can choose to move away from them. It is not always an easy process, but it is an entirely possible one. Not all victims of abuse go on to be abusers. While our blood ancestry can be a huge influence on us, most of us have access to other people. We can choose. We might reject the attitudes of one parent in favor of the other. We might look to an uncle or cousin as a role model instead. Or we might turn our attention towards other kinds of ancestry to find the figures we need outside of our gene pool.

All human relationships are flawed to some degree. However, when it comes to our friends and lovers, it is far easier to negotiate around those issues. We come to each other on an equal footing. It is difficult to transition a parent-child relationship from being one based on responsibility/power to being a relationship between equals. They will still look at you and remember when you couldn't have a poo without assistance. You will still remember when they used to tell you off. I heard through the medium of Radio 4, a beautiful piece of Hindu wisdom about parenting – that until the age of five you should just play with your children. From six to fifteen, give them discipline and structure. When they are sixteen, become their friend. I think it's an excellent idea. It's also a very long way from how western culture perceives parenthood. Just because our ancestors hold certain beliefs about parenting, does not mean we have to carry them forwards.

Broken bonds

I never met one of my grandfathers, because my mother was the product of a first marriage. I grew up with that part of my family and history missing. However, to be short a grandparent was not a personal disaster, especially as I felt far more involved with my maternal line. But what did that mean for my mother? Daughter of the 'bad father' who had let the family down. That can't have been easy to grow up with. I wonder if she was a changeling child, knowing she ought to be swapped back some day. I've watched how my son's experiences seem to have brought my mother's history into focus. The stories we make about ourselves are all works in progress, and open to change.

Death, desertion and the complexities around adoption create breaks in many bloodlines. The genetic connections are obscured, and tracing them can be difficult. For some, there is little desire to seek out birth family. For those who remember traumatic times, there can be a preference to reject and deny the 'bad blood'. However, for others, those broken links cry out to be mended, sending people on complex quests to discover where they fit in the world. I suspect every last seeker heads out with the hope that there was a good reason. They were loved, and given up reluctantly. All those children's stories about orphans make me wonder at the ways in which we construct the perfect dead parents. The dead mothers of fairy tales are compelling archetypes. Their love never wanes, their beauty is never sullied and their patience never tested by difficult daughters. Harry Potter offers an interesting addition to this kind of story. The reality if a dead parent is different though. I knew one woman who was the daughter of a suicide, and felt bitter rejection because of her father's death. Even when death isn't deliberate, that sense of abandonment can still affect people.

I realize that I think about parenting from an inherently female perspective. As a woman, I am going to know whether I've had a child or not. The only exception would be a woman who chose to donate eggs for fertility treatment, and I have no idea how a donor gets to grips with that conceptually. The donating of sperm is, I think, more widespread, but I've never talked to anyone who has admitted to doing it. If a man has sex with a woman and does not sustain the relationship, he may never know whether there was a child. I have talked to men who comment that they assume they aren't fathers because no one ever got back to them, but who wonder about it. The possibility of being a father, unknowingly, must exist in the minds of a great many men. I imagine that for some, that might be a comfort, for others, a cause for concern. I know of men who have enthusiastically claimed 'surprise' children but no doubt there are some who are less keen. I have no way of imagining, really, what it would be like for me to not know whether I had a child, and I think that is bound up in my own sense of self, and may be equally significant for others.

With so much cultural emphasis on the family, it cannot be easy not knowing who your people are, or why you aren't with them. Adoptive families can be beautiful things. That doesn't just mean formal adoption of children by adults, but the families we make for ourselves out of natural affinity and mutual care. I think each story of adoption and broken chains will be so individually circumstanced that I am loathe to generalize. Is the hunger for a place to belong keener in those who have broken lineage? It's impossible to tell. A person either grows up with the story of their blood family, or they do not. I do think that when we go in search of missing links, it is the narrative, as much as the people that we seek. The story of what happened to us, and how we came to be where we are, is one that we all need. We all need enough story to place ourselves, but what that means will vary according to the individual. The right approach is the one that makes sense.

Did we choose our ancestry?

There is a theory that we choose our parents. The idea assumes that we have a life separate from the life of the body, and that as souls we can decide where and when we can be born. Embracing this idea means choosing to believe that we have chosen this life. We have chosen these parents, these ancestors, deliberately and for some soul reason that our current consciousness is unable to access.

I can see how this idea might bring comfort. For someone whose ancestry has been a source of pain or challenge, the idea of having chosen it gives back a degree of control. The idea that the hard times may have been endured for a reason makes them easier to bear. If it is part of our mysterious soul journey, part of something we have chosen to learn for a higher purpose, then that's fine, isn't it?

The downside is that such a belief also makes us responsible for what we are going through. After all, we chose it. We opted to be here, with these people. Often the idea of choosing our parents includes a belief that we have mapped out all the major events of our life in advance. So there's no point complaining about it now. We chose to go through this. I can see a great deal to be concerned about in such a philosophy. I don't personally like the idea that we've planned it all in advance and are now just going through it. That seems pointless. It's partly my author-self speaking here, because if I plan a story in detail, I don't write it. I like there to be surprises. And ye gods, I'd like to think if I'd planned this life, I'd have done a much better job of it. I'd rather think the mistakes I've made were the consequence of youthful naivety rather than the consequence of a masochistic soul that has deliberately sought out a great deal of pain.

If the idea of having chosen your circumstances is a helpful story, then use it. If it makes you feel stronger and more able to handle the time and place in which you have landed, then all well and good. If it doesn't fit into your world view, or it makes everything look even worse than it already did, reject it. As we are entirely able to choose our beliefs, we might as well be pragmatic in selecting the ones that make it easier to live and rejecting the ones that would cause pointless pain or slow us down. Who knows? Even if some of us did choose, it might not mean everyone did. Perhaps in reincarnation, as in authoring, there are those who like to figure it out in advance, and those who like to make it up as we go along.

Working with immediate ancestors

Sometimes it is possible to sit down with an older family member and hear their versions of our stories. The sharing of memories is a bonding experience, and in happier households can be a very sweet thing to do. Where there is old wounding, it can be harder to make that first approach and to ask the all important question of 'why?'

There are times when to move forward, we have to make sense of the past. Doing this from a place of anger or resentment does not bring peace. It may be tempting to go back to an older relative and demand they apologize for what they did, for the shortcomings we perceive, or for the ways in which we feel let down by them. A hostile demand for apology tends to widen the gap rather than bringing the insight that facilitates healing. It doesn't mean allowing people off the hook and accepting their excuses, but it does call for listening to the explanations. Sometimes they can make all the difference.

I did a lot of soul searching in my twenties, and a lot of wondering about my childhood. During this process, I started emailing my father. He and I both seem to do better on paper, we both write and it's a calmer, less threatening way of communicating hard things – for me at least. I sounded him out about my impressions of how things were, and he came back with stories that were wholly new to me. These were not stories about me, but about him and his sisters, the childhood he had experienced, and the way those siblings had, in later life, started to make sense of what relations with their parents had done to their own abilities to hold relationship. All of a sudden what could have turned into a story about me, became a legacy story, a knock on from something far older. Why were my paternal grandparents relating to each other in a way that has knocked on like this? I may never answer that, although I have some ideas. Who knows how many generations back those issues might go? But they are not carrying forwards. They stop, between me and my father. They stop with us because we have managed to recognize them and speak about them. It doesn't magically fix everything, but it makes certain that my son will not have the same experiences. But it wasn't until my father had talked with his own sisters, after the death of his parents, and made a peace with his own history, that we were able to have that conversation.

It is possible to make peace with the dead. Sometimes it's

easier because they aren't in a position to argue, but I think peace in person is better. It gives us more certainty that the peace we have made is real. I never met my maternal grandfather – he remarried and had no contact with my mother either as she grew up. To the end of her life, my grandmother carried grief and resentment over that relationship, and my mother has (I believe) a private understanding of a father. Being able, finally, to connect with her paternal family has given her a great deal. But he was never there, and we never knew him. Whatever peace we make with his absence, the hole remains.

All my life, the grandfather I never met lived just a few miles from me. His second wife was, as I understood it, the one who demanded that there be no contact, and her son was the one who made contact with our side of the family. For many years, I resented the woman who had deprived me of a grandfather. It felt like an absolute injustice. This year I met her for the first time – a frail old woman showing signs of memory loss and confusion. In some ways, she reminded me so much of my grandmother that it was heart-breaking to be in proximity to her. She had no real idea of who I was, or of her own part in our shared history. There was no point being angry with her. My maternal grandparents are both dead, nothing can bring about what never was. My anger would hurt a frail, aging woman, and cause pain to my wider family. I let it go.

Much of this is about my deciding that I don't want to carry anger with me. I've seen people who blame everything in their lives on other people, and put their own inaction down to the things that have been done to them. I've also met people who have survived horrendous abuse both as adults and children, and who have not let this become the entirety of their lives. The smallest familial setbacks can be turned into reasons to not live fully. The most horrendous experiences can be overcome by people who are determined to not repeat the past and to be more than victims. Whatever experiences we have had, we can choose how to move forward and whether to make those stories the sum of our lives.

I knew a young man whose mother abandoned him when he was four, and who spent his childhood moving between foster homes. He had an absolute belief that no one could love him, and anyone who tried was therefore tested and pushed until they could no longer bear his behavior and had to retreat from it. I don't think it ever crossed his mind that there might be other ways to behave. If he had relinquished the idea that no one could stick by him, he might have given someone the chance to actually do so. The stories we derive from our pasts can so easily be traps that keep us prisoner. Only by being conscious of our own stories and the myths we create about ourselves, can we hope to take control of them.

One of the underpinning features of story is the causal link and the idea that an event means something. 'This has happened, and therefore…' Our early experiences create our ideas of what is normal, and even as adults we can be trained to accept as normal all kinds of unacceptable things. If our parents treated us in a certain way, it therefore becomes reasonable to assume that everyone else will too. We might then go on, as the young man described above did, to make sure that remains true. If we go into the world willing to change our stories to fit any new evidence coming in, we have a chance to break those old patterns. Life is not like fiction and real people are not like characters. Our personalities are far more open to change, and there is no narrative theme underpinning our lives. We are not living in a Thomas Hardy novel, written to show how grinding fate inevitably crushes the little people. We do not exist to play out ideas about jealousy, or retribution, or anything else. We absorb so much of our sense of reality from stories, it's hardly surprising that we may absorb the idea of narrative structure as well. Life does not have a narrative structure. We do not, therefore, need to invent stories for ourselves that tie us into one.

A willingness to let go of the old stories can be vital in healing relationships with our immediate ancestors, and not replicating their mistakes. We are not the sequel to their lives. Nor has the shape of our life been 'written' by our early experiences. We have the power to choose, the difficult thing is recognizing that power, and seeing the places where we can bring it to bear.

Seeking the ancestors

Looking beyond our most immediate ancestors takes a degree of effort. Family stories may shed some light upon previous generations, but these will be colored by the perceptions of the teller. My mother and grandmother told such different tales about my great grandmother that it often seemed as though they were describing two different people. In some ways they were. My grandmother referred mostly to her own childhood when her mother was much younger, my mother only knew her grandmother as an old woman.

Family legends can offer tantalizing glimpses into the past. There's a tale that one of my ancestors was an Irish heiress who ran away with a stable lad. I also know of a woman called Octavia, who went mad, and three brothers called Percival, Arthur and Lancelot. I could poke around in parish records for dates, but there won't be anything available to answer the questions that most intrigue me. Why did Octavia go mad? And why were those three brothers so named? Someone must have had very romantic inclinations. There are so many fragments. I might be able to substantiate the bare facts, but will never know the motives, or the emotions.

When it comes to genealogy, I know very little. My uncle has researched the family history at length, exploring various branches back into the past. Looking at his tree, it's mentioned clearly where he's had to make guesses about where people came from, or the ways in which surnames might have evolved with time. It's possible some of my ancestors were Jewish and came over with William the Conqueror. I'm aware of another family who set off to trace the ancestors, probably hoping to find someone with a title, or the illegitimate offspring of a king tucked away for good measure. They instead found a few young men who were hung for sheep stealing, and stopped there, the origins they discovered being uncomfortably distant from how they perceived themselves to be. The ancestors when we find them do not always confirm our sense of self.

To what extent do we root our own sense of identity in our understanding of our ancestry? Money tends to pass down through families, status and power going with it. As the middle classes came into existence, new money was shunned by old families as being coarse, and tainted by 'trade'. Being able to prove you came from older stock, mattered socially. The idea that the social standing of our parents defines us can be seen widely until relatively recently. It's still very much the case that your parents' wealth will inform your life chances more than any other single factor, but at least in theory these days we are allowed to move in different circles from our parents.

So when our historical ancestors fail to be as we expected, this can not only come as a blow, but also seem like a real threat. I think the odds are good we will all turn out to have figures in our ancestral lines who make us extremely uncomfortable. How do we relate to these figures? Do we judge them based on the standards of our time, or try to make sense of them in historical context?

For example, some of my family came from Bristol. I don't know a great deal about them as individuals, but I do know that the wealth of Bristol as a port owed a great deal to the slave trade. Even people who weren't working in it directly will have benefited from the work and wealth that most horrendous business generated. I'm certainly not aware of any ancestors who campaigned heroically against slavery. For a long time after slavery was outlawed in the UK, slave ships still used our ports, slaves came into ports like Bristol, and officially didn't leave the ships. I've seen locations where local legend has it, that slaves were indeed kept onshore. Stories of secret tunnels and pubs with chains in the basement may be anecdotal of course. From the water it is obvious that there are hidden landing places where slaves could easily have been taken. I have no idea to what extent my direct ancestors were involved, but they will have been, indirectly, at the very least.

What would I do if I came from a family whose modern wealth could readily be traced back to the slave trade? Or to some other form of colonial or industrial exploitation? What if I had a witch-finder in my family tree? To what extent are we responsible for the wrongs our ancestors have committed? Every now and then a government or some other official body apologizes for a historical atrocity. I don't know if this does any good at all, but it highlights the complexity of our relationship with the past, and with the actions of our ancestors.

Non-pagan ancestors

One of the biggest challenges for a modern pagan wishing to work with the ancestors, is the extent of non-pagan ancestry most of us have. Even if our more recent ancestors are not religious, or only mildly so, and are not affronted by our paganism, we can be confident plenty of our older ancestors would have been.

There have been times, and places, where not believing in the then-preferred interpretation of Christianity was enough to get you killed. Whether the victims of the witch hunts were genuine pagans or not, is beyond me to say, but their deaths represent a very real fear of pagan, heretical and non-Christian belief amongst our ancestors. Plenty of modern people are unable to view paganism as separate from Satanism. Many of our ancestors would have felt the same way.

If we honor our ancestors in ritual, we therefore have to

contend with the idea that many of them would hate and fear that, and might respond with anger if not actual violence were they able to participate bodily. None of us can hope to know how the entirety of our ancestors would feel about being honored in ritual, but I think we can guess that there would have been plenty for whom this would constitute an insult, at best. This of course assumes that beliefs held in life are carried across into death and that our ancestors have not magically transcended into a state consistent with a pagan world view that would cause them all to like us.

I suspect many modern pagans get round this with a little mental gymnastics. When we honor the ancestors, we honor the distant pagan ones. It's a certainty we all have those as well. It also isn't certain is how any of them would feel about what we get up to in modern rituals either. I suspect modern paganism bears little resemblance to historical forms – small details of dress and language guarantee this without even getting into the spiritual angle. What stories we have suggest that being remem-bered did matter to these ancient ancestors though. Being recorded in song and poem might be your true immortality. Perhaps they would appreciate being thought of more than they would be troubled by our methods. We can never know. We can hope, and imagine.

When we talk about our distant, pagan blood ancestry in ritual, a significant part of what we are doing isn't about honoring them, it is affirming our connection with them. We don't have clear, unbroken lineage of tradition and practice connecting us, but by thinking about them, imagining them, we hold a sense of relationship. We imagine the ancient pagan ancestors smiling benevolently upon us from the summerlands, or wherever we think they are. We reinforce our own sense of pagan-ness by underlining that connection with the pagan past.

The only trouble is that to reach those ancestors, we have to get past a lot of Christian ones first.

This raises some interesting questions about how we consider the nature of time. If time is a straight line, stretching back from us, through our kin, then the Christian ancestry is quite literally standing between us and our pagan heritage. That could be a block in a psychological sense, and if you view it as a perspective bearing literal truth, then it could be a very real impediment to any kind of relationship. Do we 'get passed' that Christian heritage, or do we seek ways to engage with it?

For a pagan who has rejected the immediate authority of Christianity, the idea of anything other than hostility towards Christian ancestors can be challenging. It's tempting, and not unusual to position those Christians, contemporary and historical, as other than us, and see them as adversaries. They are the ones who oppressed the original pagans, burned the witchy grannies, and tried to stamp us out. That's just another myth amongst many. A casual glance in the direction of folk magic shows that for many people historically, Christianity rubbed alongside a belief in magic and a spirit world. Many of our ancestors will have viewed themselves as Christian whilst doing things that manifestly had nothing at all to do with that religion.

I don't think we can afford to ignore our Christian ancestors. It does not serve us to wish them away. Again, we do not know them as individuals; we do not know what they thought or felt, or exactly how any of them might have responded to us. We can therefore choose how we relate to them. It makes sense to me to bring what empathy and compassion we can to our perceptions of the past.

After all, perhaps time is not a wholly linear thing. Perhaps we are not as far away from our ancestors as we imagine. We do not know, in the great metaphysical scheme of things, what odds our perceptions might make. In terms of ourselves, it is apparent that carrying forward resentment will not do us any good. It will not bring peace, or grant fulfillment, and it certainly won't help us deal with non-pagan contemporaries. Where our ancestors were human, it would be as well not to hold that against them.

Deep ancestry and creative connections

I once heard Emma Restall Orr speaking about 'the grand-mothers' as a notion of ancestors. It's a lovely, resonant word, full of the warmth of fairy tale grandmothers, and the iconography of the witchy granny. It gives us something broad, distant, and strong to work with. Not just your own immediate grand-mothers, but the totality of grandmother-hood. I remember a spring some time after that, walking in the woods and looking at the bluebells. Each flower a distinct individual, making up a vast sea of blue, full of more flowers than I could count. I looked at them, and I thought 'the grandmothers are like this'.

It may be because of my gender, or the knowledge that there were some difficult men in my family a few generations ago, but 'the grandfathers' took a little longer to get to grips with. I found them through a long winter, living in a house that one of my grandfathers had grown up in. I gained a sense of how hard life was, living close to the land, and how much strength and physical effort the normal work of laboring men must have called for. The grandfathers came to personify strength and effort, and became something I could draw inspiration from. At the same time, the literal grandfathers were the sort of people to decide that an old radiator would make an entirely adequate covering for a well. I learned to find a balance between the two under-standings.

Once we step beyond the stories we know, our ancestors of blood become both numerous and vague. They become the grandmothers and grandfathers, and although bits of them live on in us, we will seldom know in what ways they manifest. It's easy for the deep ancestors to also be fantasy ancestors. We can only know them through imagination and intuition, which makes it easy for us to fit them into our stories in whatever way suits us.

On one hand, having a sense of deep ancestry and connection

to our distant blood lines can be healing and stabilizing. They give us a sense of belonging to a wider family, even if our immediate one is less than perfectly comfortable, or not even available to us. They are the ones who have seen and known everything, they are the bearers of wisdom and whatever we may face, we can be sure they have endured it too. Nothing is new.

My own sense of deep ancestry connected directly with finding the place where some of those ancestors had lived. Being in a house that had belonged to my family for eight generations, gave me a tangible link to the past. They were in the walls and the floorboards – literally to some degree. Although by this I mean more their dust and sweat than actual bodies! They had built and rebuilt the building, were born, lived, worked and died within it. They had farmed the land, given their blood and sweat to the soil. The local cemetery held their bodies, and I was able to wander amongst them, wondering exactly how many of the folk there I had a connection with.

I find the company of the dead very soothing. Graveyards in the area I grew up in are especially resonant, because I know there will be ancestors there. Not recent ones though. My grandmother's grave is still too painful and immediate, but there's a calmness to being with the long dead. All of the troubles and trials they knew have gone into the soil with them.

How we relate to the more ancient dead depends a lot on how we relate to time and ideas of the afterlife. If time is linear and there is no afterlife, then the dead are gone and unavailable. We might see them instead as spirits who continue in some other realm, available to be called upon at times of need. Some cultures do venerate their ancestors because they are perceived as being closer to the gods and able to intervene on behalf of their descendants. If time is not a straight line, or if ghosts are real, then the ancestors may be alongside us. Even if they are truly gone, we may experience their echoes, the resonance of them in the places they once inhabited.

There are a great many ways in which we can choose to understand our relationship with our ancestors, and no reason to think any of them more sensible than any other. It is a matter of preference, intuition and inclination. We may choose to envisage our older ancestors as too distant to be known, and irrelevant to our own lives. We may feel them as a close presence and a benevolent force. How we relate to them is a consequence of how we perceive history, and the stories we tell to ourselves about the nature of time and reality.

There are some people who believe that reincarnation happens specifically within families, and that we return to the people we came from, in new bodies. If this is so, then the events of the past are very relevant indeed for the present. Other schools of thought around reincarnation imagine us re-encountering the same souls, but not necessarily with that clear family focus. Where belief is in an afterlife rather than a return, those ancestors might be imagined to be waiting for us wherever we go next. Or the ancestors may indeed meld into one pool of ancestral energy, full of wisdom and compassion that we can tap into.

I'm in the curious position that I do not have any fixed beliefs about any of this. I have no idea what happens when we die, although I like the notion of reincarnation. There are also days when I like the idea of this life being it, and am horrified by the notion of being stuck with me for all eternity. There have been times when my more distant ancestors have felt like a real and protective presence in my life, and times when that has seemed like a self-indulgent fantasy. I have no idea if they wait around after death, or if they cease to exist, but I still talk to them. I find it comforting to sit with them. At a time in my life when I was in great need and felt very vulnerable, my family came through for me, and I had six months of living in the home of my ancestors. That was a profound experience with real impact on my life. Were my ancestors with me through that hard time, in any literal sense? I don't know. I like to think they were.

I've already written considerably about the issue of choosing what we believe, and the scope we have to consciously construct our own myths and stories. I'm equally conscious of my own resistance to this as an idea. I have developed a distinct personal aversion to ascribing meaning to anything I experience. Exposure to the psychotic and dysfunctional beliefs of others has made me wary of anything I cannot explain. A desire to be taken seriously has encouraged me to avoid anything I can't substantiate. Alongside that, I also have a personal fear of being considered insane if I express anything outside of mainstream perception.

Belief is irrational. It is very precisely about relating to things we have no proper evidence for. Taking anything other than academic interest in our more distant ancestors, is irrational. Believing we can have any kind of meaningful relationship with them suggests a less than perfectly sensible mind. A life that is stripped down to what is proven, reliable and reasonable, is a life that becomes thin and narrow. Inspiration is not rational. Love is not rational. In most regards, humans are not rational. The idea of needing a lot of evidence to justify belief would probably make no sense at all to most of my ancestors. But here I am nonetheless, exploring as theoretical possibilities things I am, at time of writing, unable to feel. I promised early in the book to flag up those things pertaining to myself that impact directly on my own ability to interpret, and I think this is one of them – my own ambivalence around belief and anything I can't substantiate. While my ancestors undoubtedly existed, I can't confidently assert much about them beyond that. There's a tension here, between fact and imagination, between need and knowledge, and that fascinates me. There are lines to walk between intuition and insanity, which are a constant issue for anyone exploring deeper pagan practices. How much of what we experience can we afford to claim as real?

As soon as we reach out towards the deep ancestry, we move from the safe subjects of genealogy and philosophy, into something more immediate, more personal, and more open to the most self-serving and irrational impulses within us.

I could meditate upon my deep ancestors and 'discover' that I am descended from a long line of ancient Druids. I could 'know' their wisdom because it would all be in my blood line, all there for me to grasp intuitively. I could cast myself as the one true inheritor of all things ancient and Druidic, and stride forth into the world to proclaim myself as very, very important. I wouldn't be the first pagan to make such claims. I have no idea whether anyone who has set themselves up as an inheritor truly believes it, or is acting cynically.

In practice, I've never delved into my deep ancestry looking for any kind of Druids, and if I found them, I would be too conscious of my own yearnings to be trustful, and would be unlikely to even mention it in public. In this, perhaps I err too far the other way. Perhaps we should be listening to the voices of our deep ancestry. Perhaps all the ancient Druids are there on the other side, just waiting for us to hear them. I am personally unable to believe in anything so straightforward. If it was that simple, someone brighter and better than me would have done it already, or we would all wake up the morning after our initiation with it right there, shining inside our heads, burning on our brows... Whatever ancient Druidry is, or was, it doesn't seem inclined to magically turn up, and I have a feeling if it did, most of us wouldn't understand it anyway. If it turned up in ancient Welsh, most of us wouldn't stand a chance.

Instead, when I have meditated on deep ancestry, or sought for guidance, it's been of a much broader sort. The simple 'how do I survive?' questions that have been so essential for all those generations. I've looked for strength and endurance, the will to keep going, a sense of connection and belonging to hold me firm during stormy times. I've been reaching for the grandmothers, for friendly faces and reassurance. There have been times when I felt that I had found it, or encountered something real. Often, late at night, contemplating the rich mud of the flood plain and the presence of ancestral bones within that mud has brought me a profound sense of connection. They have not told me how to live my life, or how to be a better sort of Druid. Nothing so specific or detailed. I wouldn't have trusted it, if they had.

Mine is at present a story about doubt and uncertainty, in which I would resist anything unsubstantiated as being possible evidence of delusion on my part. At the same time I am aware of the potential for entirely different stories, and curious to see if, during the ongoing process of writing, researching and contemplating this book, my sense of reality shifts at all.

Chapter Seven

Ancestors of Place

Whatever stories they may have had died with them... Romano British... Angles ... Heathens... we wonder what body of land-stories may have once existed ... We wonder too at what stories we, and others, could create anew to reinvest the spirit in the Sacred Land.[38]

'Place' is an idea we can contemplate very broadly, or specifically as we prefer. On the whole I think it makes most sense to consider ancestors of place in terms of the people and others associated with the places we are now using. Go back a few generations and, for the majority, ancestors of place would have included a fair number of blood kin. These days, with increased mobility, living somewhere you have no historical connection with is far more normal. We frequently do not work where we live, and will also travel for our religious commitments and leisure pursuits. As a consequence, there might be a large number of places with which we have a connection, and whose previous occupants therefore hold interest for us.

Ancestors of place have the positive function of helping us connect to where we are, in any aspect of our lives. For someone who has been uprooted, by choice, necessity or force, making new connections with a new place is a great aid to emotional wellbeing. When I moved from the area I had grown up in, I spent a lot of time trying to find out the history and folklore of the place I had moved to. The Cotswold home of my childhood was a landscape luscious with story. It was only after moving I realized that had been important for me. Being in a place where I had no stories to help root me in my surroundings, left me feeling dislocated and unhappy. As Robin Herne observes, 'Knowing that past generation of your bloodline have lived in a place gives a unique sense of belonging to the land, being somehow part of it.'[39]

The town I had moved to, was a new town largely constructed in the sixties, although some parts of it were much older. There wasn't much folklore, and it took me a long time to build up a good body of stories. My own tales became part of that mythmaking, alongside details I gleaned from friends. Having a narrative of place gives us a relationship with our surroundings. From a Druidic point of view, this is very important. If we have no relationship with the land, it is harder to treat it with love and respect. People who feel no sense of connection with their surroundings are far more likely to mistreat them. To perceive the soul of a place, to value it and to feel for it, does not come automatically. Having a narrative enables us to make this journey, and also to help others connect as well.

As a traveler, my first interest is always in the stories associated with a place. Wandering around in the UK, there is a huge variety in quantity of available story. Some places are resplendent with it. Half an hour in a museum or poking around in a church leads to a wealth of insight about people and events. In other places, there's very little. However, that can be rectified. I knew several storytellers from the Birmingham area who were in the process of creating new urban myths. They were mixing known historical details with imagination, creating tales rooted in the immediate landscape, but entirely recent in their construction. If those stories manage to travel, they will become folklore, given time. I don't think the lack of age matters at all. Places need stories. Or at least, people need stories about places. If those stories do not already exist the answer is to make them up as best you can.

One of the narratives that particularly affected me in this regard is Neil Gaiman's Neverwhere. It works with the names of stations in the London underground, creating characters and myths around them. I'm not aware of any specific folklore drawn on in this work of fiction – but the idea of creating stories out of names or features is not anything new. Much of the folklore we have is very precisely that – a means of explaining something. And so ancient rabbit warrens become plague graves, hill forts become Roman chariot racing places, and Silbury Hill becomes the result of a cunning ploy to distract the Devil from going to Salisbury. Playing with names, Bromsgrove becomes Brom's grave, and Brom himself a giant who strides across the West Midlands. I have no idea how old that story is. Similarly I've heard people assume that 'bury' in a name indicated an ancient burial place. In fact it is Saxon and to do with fortifications. The etymology of place names can give us glimpses of real stories, but the sounds of names can equally furnish us with the raw material to make new ones.

When we go looking for our ancestors of place, one of the things to bear in mind is that those ancestors were story-makers too. The stories they leave may well be vibrant and exciting, but won't necessarily have a shred of historical truth in them. The Roman chariot track story is a fine example – it is a story belonging to Uley Bury in Gloucestershire, and I heard it from my grandmother. Allegedly, the earthworks were an old chariot race track. Anyone walking the old hill fort can see at a glance that only the suicidal would attempt to race anything round the narrow path with its tight corners. I suspect the myth of having a great deal to do with the film Ben Hur and far more recent ancestors reinterpreting the landscape in light of what they'd seen on the big screen.

Most of the UK has seen continuous habitation for thousands of years. We have field systems that are dated to the Iron Age[40] and other landscape features that are the consequence of prolonged interaction between people and the land. Our dramatic fells would have been tree covered, and far less visually striking, were it not for centuries of grazing sheep, encouraged by their human owners. Ancestry of place can give us more direct access to the distant past, with ancient remains being a real and influential presence. It also raises questions around ownership, and the way in which we prioritize human ruins and influences in the landscape.

We have a fascination with the remains of former cultures and, by human standards, this is a fairly new thing. It seems to belong to the past few hundred years, antiquarians and the origins of archaeology. I also suspect faster travel and increased leisure time for tourism of playing a part. Once there was reason to think human history might have more in it than the details recorded by the Old Testament, we've become a lot more curious about our past. At first, perhaps wanting to prove or disprove the stories we have heard, and increasingly with a desire to extend our understanding of the human condition.

In the UK we now go to considerable lengths to preserve old buildings and ancient monuments and to avoid interfering with them. This, as an obsession, is twentieth century in origin. Ancestors only a little prior to that had no qualms about rearranging stone circles, borrowing stone from them for other building work, plowing over antiquities, and knocking down old buildings to make way for new ones. We may have gone too far the other way with a fixation on preservation that turns many buildings into museum pieces and makes it hard to continue their use. Planning laws mean sometimes people will opt to let a building fall down because they cannot afford to restore it in the appropriate way, which is wasteful and pointless. Even modern features added to old houses can be hard to change if your property is a listed building.

We cling to evidence of the past for all kinds of reasons – for its beauty, for the history associated with it, for what we hope to learn, and other reasons perhaps to do with nostalgia, or a fear of letting go. The rush of ugly post-war construction may also be part of what inspires us to hang onto buildings that were made with more love, and less concrete. Yet now even the sixties monstrosities seem open to preservation orders. In clinging to the places humans have created, we cling also to those ancestors of place, and perhaps keep something of them alive and present by keeping their buildings. These signs of our ancestors give them a kind of immortality, and perhaps it is our own fear of disappearing into obscurity that makes us inclined to keep evidence of our predecessors intact.

In terms of tourism, the ancestors of place have given us a significant industry. Any historical event or remnant can be capitalized upon and turned into an attraction. We will happily pay a lot of money to clamber round the ruins of our ancestors' homes, to ponder the inevitable small walls archaeology exposes, and to look at artistic interpretations of how it might have been. Reconstructed rooms and costumed re-enactments draw us as well – not just historical remnants, but recreations that may give us a 'flavor'. So it isn't necessarily the scope for directly connecting with ancient things that appeals to us. If we visit a reconstruction, what exactly are we engaging with? Is our best guess at how the past looked more, or less, informative than the small remains history may have offered us?

Kevan Manwaring ponders the same issue in Turning the Wheel: 'Why do people re-enact? Is it a past life thing? A way of connecting with and honoring ancestors?'[41]

The ancestors of place are both present and impersonal. We focus on the ones who have left evidence of their presence, but we don't have to deal with them so personally as we do with our immediate blood ancestors, making them much more readily adaptable to suit our needs. However, as with the ancestors of blood, most of the people who lived in the places we now occupy, are not immediately visible to us. Some can be found with closer inspection, but the majority are elusive. The further back we go, the fewer traces remain. Some places have their Bronze and Stone

Age remnants, but most have little direct evidence to show of human occupation, even if we do suspect they were there. Partly this is because we build over the old places. Sites evolve over time, find new uses, and the history becomes so many layers under the soil, hidden from view.

Archaeology can get down through the layers and tell us about the hidden past. The trouble is that in so doing, it tends to dismantle. This is an issue I find problematic. Torn between the desire to know, and the desire to preserve, our current levels of technology make it hard to do both at the same time and in the same place. Once items are found, they tend to leave the site of their origin, taking out of the landscape the remnants of those ancestors of place whose presence we were inspired by. I think when we have a sense that the people in the soil are our people, something changes. When we feel that connection as personal – for whatever reasons – our own sense of belonging to a place is intensified by it.

The relationship between ancestral remnants, study, the landscape and our communities is a vast and complex one, which I will be coming back to in more detail later in this book.

Non-human ancestry in the landscape

When it comes to considering ancestors of place, there is every reason to pay attention to our non-human ancestry. Trees in our landscapes can have their roots stretched considerably into the past, reaching back through centuries. They are living ancestors, their presence having helped shape the places we now experience. Their own ancestors in the forests of distant history will have provided the fuel and building tools our ancestors depended on, remnants of which may still be visible in older houses. The ways in which plants distribute themselves, creatures distribute plants, and creatures change their environments all contributes to shaping the world we see.

Otters use the same holts over many generations. Rookeries

and other roosting sites can be far longer lived than the inhabitants. Beavers dam up rivers, alder trees create swamps if left to their own devices. We are not the only force at work in the countryside, and though human activity may seem to dominate, the story is a far more complex one, once we start looking at it. The relationships between plants, soil and water flows can be hugely influential in terms of crafting the landscape. The presence of ancient trees buried in the earth has resulted in a coal industry that defines some areas economically, visually and socially. Bodies of countless ancient sea creatures give us limestone rock – and in the Cotswolds, that limestone forms our hills and permeates our drinking water. We are literally walking on the bodies of our ancient ancestors. Everywhere there is soil, there are countless ancestors of place whose deaths have gone into making up the fertile part of the land. Our food depends upon them.

Where buildings dominate the landscape, it can be difficult to imagine the presence of any non-human ancestry. However, our constructions are all recent in the great scheme of things. Somewhere underneath the tarmac, there is soil. It may seem that modern roads and cities are purely human constructions, made to serve our purposes, but these too are shaped by land and history. Towns will, for example, form where once it was easy to ford the river with livestock.

Research into the history and origins of a place can give us some idea about the non-human ancestry involved in the landscape. It frequently also calls for a degree of imagination, and a willingness to look beyond purely human concerns.

As soon as we start exploring the issue of non-human ancestry, it becomes apparent how much has gone that was once here. In England, the inhabitants have changed considerably since the last ice age. Gone are the saber-toothed tigers, the woolly rhinos and the small elephants, along with all the other exotic creatures who weren't equipped to cope with changes in the climate. We used to have beavers, wolves, bears, wild boar, cranes, pelicans, aurochs, and no doubt many others who have been wiped out by human activity. The red squirrels are on the brink, our otters were nearly annihilated, and many of our smaller creatures are close to disappearing. Even some of the domestic creatures we humans carefully developed through generations of selective breeding are in danger too, along with so many of our native apple breeds. They depend on us entirely for survival, but we are letting them go because they are no longer all that useful. Once the heavy horses were commonplace work animals, but their numbers are dwindling.

Some of our lost ancestor creatures continue in other countries. In the cases of beavers and cranes, considerable breeding and reintroduction programs are under way, but I can't see bears or wolves making a comeback. Not least because their habitats are too greatly reduced. Having wiped out all non-human potential threats, I can't imagine we as a species, are going to let them back in again, sadly.

Of all the non-human ancestors, it is the loss of the aurochs that haunts me most. These giant, wild cattle are now entirely extinct. The last one died, I believe, in Poland in the sixteen hundreds. By all accounts they stood some two meters high, and wandered grazing through the woods and marshes of ancient England. Extinction is always a tragedy. For me, these lost creatures have also become icons of the lost landscape, of the wild places capable of supporting such huge mammals. When I find somewhere a little wild and remote, it is the absence of aurochs that I most often think about.

The role of humans as ancestors of place is therefore not an entirely comfortable or straightforward one. It is our human ancestors of place who have driven out our non-human ancestors, hunted them to extinction or ruined their habitats. It was our human ancestors of place who felled forests and cut the landscape up with ever-more intrusive road systems. Our ancestors of place erected the ugly, soulless buildings that still dominate so many cities, built bleak factories and slum dwellings and poisoned our water systems. Looking at the enormous electricity pylons striding across and defacing this landscape, I know I can thank my ancestors of place for them as well.

The ancestors were also those who worked with the trees, developing the many apple varieties that are now in such danger of being lost. They also drained the marshes, creating valuable farmland, but at a cost to the waterfowl and other marsh residents pushed to the margins as a consequence. Ancestors of place dug the canals, which I love, and built the ever noisy motorway, which I hate passionately, as it divides the river from the hills. My ancient ancestors could have walked freely, where I cannot because of this road, this desire for speed and convenience that chops up the land, and divides the people within it.

Thinking about the non-human ancestors of places makes it clear that we cannot consider the human ones as a single, straightforward group. Not only are they the builders and creators, they are also the wreckers and despoilers. For every ancestor who left a legacy of beauty there will be another who ruined something irrevocably.

In embracing our non-human ancestry, we open ourselves to considering all kinds of thing as being part of our heritage. We might think of those creatures who have been farmed to the benefit of our human ancestors, and upon whom our blood ancestors depended for all manner of resources. This shift in thinking enables us to consider our own position in new ways. We are not purely inheritors of the human influence upon the landscape. We also inherit the legacy of trees, the influence of grazing livestock, we become descendants of the rookery, people of the animal paths. We can revalue the many non-humans around us alongside doing this, recognizing that 'place' is far more than people.

As a culture we would rush to preserve any site that humans

have used for a thousand years, yet feel little such compunction when it comes to the sites that non-humans depend on. This is in part because we see our own history as being distinct and separate from that of other living things, and more important than it. They say it is the victors who write the history books. That invariably means humans, of one sort or another. The stories we tell are almost exclusively from our own narrow perspective, and encourage us to continue in the same vein, treating all other living things as secondary. We say that the aurochs became extinct. We do not say that we wiped them out, along with a lot of other creatures. 'Became extinct' sounds so much more neutral, an inevitable, accidental, unfortunate thing, a footnote in the history of human progress.

As we construct our myths and our stories of the past, we position ourselves in relation to all other living things. Many of our human history stories contain only the barest references to non-human presences. They come into the tale as foodstuffs and trade items, as modes of transport and symbols of wealth, but even then, only fleetingly. We seldom give sufficient thought even to these critical roles.

I once ran into the suggestion that humans did not domesticate dogs. They domesticated us. Sadly I cannot recall either the details of the argument or the source of it, but the idea stayed with me because it turns on its head that basic assumption that humans are always the movers and shakers creating the story. Dogs domesticated us. They came to our fires as scavengers, and adopted us into their packs, perhaps finding uses for our opposable thumbs, and the neat things we could do by rubbing sticks together. I'm sure cats domesticated us as well. Once we started storing grain, and attracting rodents, the cats would have had reason to move in, and why not sleep in front of our fires, and on our beds? We assume human authority in stories of domestication, but it may not always have been so. There are always other stories to tell, and if we can make them even slightly less human-centric, if we can imagine ourselves as a part of this world, not the natural rulers of it, we can change everything else that we do.

The idea of our ancestry being separate from that of creatures is Euro-centric and Judeo-Christian. Native Americans take a wholly different view – 'particular clans are descended from specific animals.'[42] Given folklore from around the world about shape shifting, I imagine that many traditional cultures have had a more complex attitude to our relationship with non-humans than current white, western thinking offers.

In the history of making stories about the past, there is a long tradition of ignoring a large percentage of the human population too. Traditionally history as a taught subject was all about rulers and dates. Schools instructed us in the political, economic and martial history of our own country. This can be part of deliberate political policy, as suggested by the ongoing and enthusiastic attempts by politicians to interfere with school curriculums. For example, '...calls made by Conservative politicians for a revised history curriculum that would emphasize 'British Values'... focusing on 'glorious leaders...'[43] It's only very recently that women have been put back in the history books at all. Queens may always have had a mention, but the lives of most women had no place in his-story. An increasing interest in social history has meant a far greater inclusion of women and children, people who were not in the landed, ruling elite, indigenous people, gay people, those who had previously been marginalized. In time perhaps we will also come to view 'natural history' as part of our own context and the shared history of this planet.

Race and culture

We construct ourselves partly in relation to the race we imagine we belong to, and the culture of the country we are in. Ideas of nationhood are built very much on ideas of ancestors of place. How we do this depends partly on how we understand place. If your place is a village, someone from the next village is 'not from round here'. If you view yourself as a European, or a citizen of the world, then your history, and your culture, are far broader and more inclusive, at least potentially.

For many people in the western world, ideas of race have a lot to do with skin color, where white and not-white creates the most influential divisions. Acts of 'ethnic cleansing' continue around the world, where details of racial and cultural background are given more importance than shared humanity and a right to life. Race and culture are issues we, as a species, kill over. Yet they are largely human constructs. Our ancestors of blood tell us that we have more genetic material in common than not. Why do we place so much emphasis on our belonging to certain places and claiming shared ancestors of place?

Countries do not exist. They are made from the lines human beings draw on maps. Countries exist in our heads, they are not real in any discernible sense beyond that. There is some argument for saying that countries represent cultural groupings where they have been formed by choice. Many countries have had their borders created by arbitrary, foreign judgments, gathering together peoples with nothing in common.

Countries also give cultural groupings access to physical resources, the defense of which may be deemed important for survival. The pragmatic desire to safeguard resources makes plenty of sense, but the stories we build around it are much more complicated. We talk about 'national character' as though millions of people would have something in common there. So many jokes depend on shared beliefs about people who come from different parts of the world. In English jokes, the Scots are mean, the Irish foolish, and the Welsh untrustworthy. In American jokes, Jewish people are tight with money, and French people are stupid. I imagine most countries have a set of these culturally-informed jests, each meant to show the superiority of said country. Such jokes depend entirely on stereotyping.

History tends to focus on countries, especially in the way in which it is taught to children. The history of your own country comes first. In time, you may explore the history of other countries. A glance along a library bookshelf is all it takes to make it plain that history is very much about ancestors of place. A history not at all about borders is not an easy thing to imagine, but that does not mean it could not exist.

Ownership of the land is tremendously important to our current societies. For a long time, leadership and land ownership went together, and in the UK, one of the final restrictions to be removed from universal male suffrage was the requirement to own land or property. Those who own the land control access to it and can determine the ways in which it is used. Those who own the land also own whatever of the past is manifest within the land. They own the ancestors. This has meant colonials have felt entirely entitled to take ancestral remains from colonized countries, for their own purposes.

Currently in England, working in the city and having a weekend home in the country is a popular thing to do if you are wealthy. It pushes up house prices in rural areas, but as owners of second homes pay less council tax on them, it disadvantages local authorities. Weekenders do not put their children in local schools or their money into local enterprise. Through ownership of the land, they are able to appropriate the lifestyles, histories and landscapes of rural people. Former working buildings and old shops become residences, whilst keeping the names. British villages are full of them, while young people from poorer rural families are pushed towards cheaper lives in built-up areas, and pushed into places they have no historical connection with. The countryside is increasingly the retreat of the rich, turning the recent history of working people into heritage centers and quaint attractions. In Wales for a time, local people were so sick of the English invasion of their villages, that they took to burning holiday cottages.

When we think about race and culture, it is important to consider how real, immediate and personal those ideas are. The 'citizen of the world' idea may be appealing in its inclusivity, but having a small place to belong can be of far greater emotional significance. Race is a story we tell and has far more to do with who we imagine our ancestors to be than any kind of reality. Race is largely a myth, but immediate family and place are very present within our lives. As we've moved away from tribes towards larger and more centralized cultures, we've lost some of the immediacy of ancestry of place. Economic pressures to move may mean we live in places we have no stories about, and no relationship with. These days, supporting the local football team might be the closest any of us can get to a sense of tribal belonging.

Every place has its own character and energy. It comes from the present occupants, from the history of use, building and development, from the relationship with the landscape and climate. Individual towns have cultures and specific accents. They have their own histories and traditions.

Ideas of nationhood divide us, focusing on the differences, the conflicts and the barriers. At the same time, ancestors of place who belong to huge geographical areas, are impersonal and unreal. When it comes to ancestors of place and our constructs of race and culture, the green adage 'think global, act local' has huge potential. We are all citizens of the world, and people who exist in a very specific and immediate culture. That which is closest to us has the most capacity to ground, shape and define our lives.

Global awareness alerts us to responsibility that goes far beyond our immediate environments. We buy internationally, and our waste is disposed of by equally complex and far reaching means. The air we pollute in one country has to be breathed in all the others too. Two of our most essential assets, our air and water, cannot be owned as land is. We share them, and in recognizing our global citizenship, we could better manage those vital resources.

If we think of our race not in terms of skin color nor the place our parents came from, but to some degree in terms of our immediate ancestors of place, we have more room to belong. We can recognize that those around us belong as well, because they are here and human. Or not human even. If we make our culture immediate, root it in the place we inhabit, and not in some fantasy notion of a country, then we can have something real. The culture of a town is ours to participate in, and even shape. At that level, our actions can make a difference. When we talk about the culture of a country, we are describing an idea about an idea. It is too big and too vague to mean anything, too distant to challenge, too all-embracing to actually embrace anything meaningful at all.

The one thing that most calls into play our sense of national belonging, is war. For a Druid who is interested in peace, this relationship is disquieting.

Live locally, and claim your ethnicity as 'human.'

Cultural appropriation or gesture of respect?

If you are living in a land that was not the home of your ancestors, you have the possibility of reverencing the ancestors of the indigenous people and honoring them as your own. By this logic, a white European in Australia can honor the aboriginal ancestors. A modern white American Druid can honor the Native American ancestors and traditions. With the considerable scope now for international movement, people from any place can in theory move to, and claim the ancestors of, another place.

To what degree does living in a place make us the natural inheritors of tradition in that place? To what degree can we honorably claim these ancestors?

I know of a young woman who came to the UK from South America because she had a huge attraction to the ancient sites of this land. She considers herself pagan and is very attracted to stone circles. She clearly felt no difficulty in claiming this as part of her own heritage and expected to be treated equally with all other pagans, including those whose claim to these ancestors of place is much older. There was another girl in my first grove, of obvious African descent and from her accent I assume she wasn't born in the UK. A white American man joining the same grove a few years later found himself equally welcome and accepted. Although I don't know much about them, there are pagan groups with a far more fascist or protectionist agenda who see European-derived spirituality as very much the property of those who are much more rooted in the place. Ideas of ownership are always uncomfortable, for me.

We know some of the historical inhabitants of Europe did move round a fair bit. There is Viking graffiti in the Hagia Sophia, the Romans got themselves over most of the continent and the many wars down the centuries moved people about all over the place, as has trade, diplomacy, slavery and other aspects of human life. How long must your people have been in a place for you to be able to claim the ancestors you believe were also active in that place? The idea of excluding someone from Druidry or paganism because they come from some other place, seems like a nonsense, but on the flip side, the habit of white 'spiritual' people appropriating the beliefs and customs of native people who have been overrun, is not straightforward.

Identity, place, tradition, race and culture are not easy threads to pick apart. The taking and using of particularly Native American culture by white people is an on-going issue that can cause a lot of resentment. There is a world of difference between processes of assimilation and integration, where cultures merge organically, and appropriation, where those in power take cultural aspects from those they have disempowered, and use them as their own. There is an aspect of humiliation and disre-spect inherent in this kind of taking. The history here is long and messy. We should not overlook the fact that white ancestors went to some lengths to try to exterminate Native American cultures, and that of other indigenous peoples around the world, and killed many individuals in the process. Christianity and European languages have been imposed on many indigenous populations. Children from numerous cultures were taken away and 'educated' in ways that denied them their own heritage, language and people. Now the descendants of the oppressors want to make off with the spiritual aspects that have survived, to use them for their own ends.

Perhaps one of the worst offenders in this regard is the 'pick and mix' attitude of some New Age folks. The kind of mentality that will happily dangle a dream catcher over the statue of Egyptian deity and stand before it to go through a few chakra cleaning exercises. While I see much to be gained from the inspiration we may find in other cultures, there is a world of difference between respectful learning, and random borrowing. All spiritual practices exist in a context and belong to a specific world view. Culture, history, language, law, and social structure all interact with religions through time, and trying to pick bits out of the mix is not necessarily productive. Borrowing spiritual practices with no thought for that context in the assumption that it can all be thrown together in one big, happy, workable mix is at best misguided.

It is a mistake to even be thinking about 'native peoples' as though they, like nations, can be characterized by one attitude, one outlook. Every person is an individual, engaging with their own traditions on their own terms and in their own ways. I have no doubt there are people all over the world who are happy to share traditional knowledge with other people who want to learn more about their ancestors of place. I also believe very strongly that we have no right to appropriate those ancestors as our own. This does raise interesting issues for Druids who are not genetically Celtic. Some ethnically and spiritually Celtic Druids are offended by those who take inspiration from Druidry without embracing the whole thing. But what is the whole thing? And who has the right to define the boundaries? I'm not certain clear answers would ever be available for this. The best we can do is tread carefully, and mindfully, offer respect and listen properly.

There is a great deal of difference between honoring and appropriation. Honoring recognizes the existence of those who went before. It pays respect to them, acknowledges their influence and importance. It does not take or seek to own. The ancestors of place are simply those who were there before us, and in this regard we have relationship with them, we are influenced by them and may be inspired by what we know of them. But that does not mean they belong to us. When we think about more distant ancestors, we choose how we relate to them, but they have no direct say in the connection. They are not able to speak to us directly in ways we cannot ignore if it does not suit us. For some, the experience of inviting ancestral presences into the circle creates real insight, but as in all things, it is important to remain vigilant against self-important ego-feeding ideas.

As Druids, we should make respect the core of every relationship we have. When we deal with the ancestors of place, not only do we need to respect them, but we must also be careful to respect descendants of blood and tradition who may feel their claim is stronger than ours. We do not honor the ancestors by offending their other descendants. For example, when exploring a church I believe is on a pre-Christian site, I would not assume the right to carry out ritual on behalf of my pagan ancestors. All those Christian ancestors of place and their inheritors of tradition have rights too. A more co-operative, collaborative approach might instead gift me with the opportunity to build connections. I might still get to do my ritual, but in a spirit of inclusion and peace, rather than as a source of pain and anger.

One of the considerations when thinking about the faith of our ancestors of place, is to what degree religion is something we do, and to what degree it defines who we are. It's often a very individual answer. When spirituality is part of a threatened cultural identity, any borrowing of it can be distressing. It can be a diminishing, a taking away. Religions that go out to recruit are of course happy to have people come onboard from any background. This perhaps has given many westerners the belief that other religions are the same, and are delighted by the prospect of new converts. The idea of conversion is part of a world view not everyone shares. If religion is what binds your community together, if it is private, and part of self, than someone trying to join in, is an invader not a happy new member of your spiritual group.

Looking for ancestors of place

Some of our ancestors of place made it into the history books and the local museums. Places that were caught up in political events, or wars, or were the birthplace of someone famous may have a few details in the local tourist guide. Even in this situation, the majority of ancestors remain invisible. We won't find them on Wikipedia either.

Our recent ancestors are often available through photographs. It's tremendously evocative, pouring over real images from another era. Details of home, costume and landscape can all be on display. Some of my own ancestors I know only from the images in a local history book. Having faces to look at makes those ancestors of the last hundred years or so come alive. Again, this will not give us much of our full scale of ancestry.

One of the books that has most helped me look for ancestral presences in the landscape is Oliver Rackham's History of the Countryside, about the history of Britain's landscape, flora and fauna. I have no idea if any comparable texts exist for other countries, and the discipline of landscape history is a rather small one. In a landscape that has seen human use for thousands of years, there are all kinds of signs and features that can give us clues about what went on in the area beforehand. I spend a lot of time walking and cycling, always with an eye for the features I know about. Woodbanks, old rabbit warrens, old trees in young woods, depths of lanes and so forth all give me hints. One of the things that fascinates me is that apparently the number of tree species in a hedge roughly equates to the age, in centuries, of said hedge. However, more environmentally aware planting schemes will make that less useful as a measure in the future.

I can't see the ancestors in any literal sense. I won't find their names, or the details of their way of life, but I can see where they have been. The local barrows give me clues that go right back to the Bronze Age. My greatest sense of ancestors of place has come from walking in the landscape. It's not just a matter of seeking out obvious ancient features either. Seeing how one village connects to the next, how you can move between the hills and the river, where the wind blows, where the rain clouds gather, I know I am seeing a landscape that has not changed since humans were first here. The modern overlay seems very thin sometimes, with the deep mud of the ancestors just beneath the surface.

Inevitably, once we get away from the history books and museum exhibits, and what can be gleaned from the etymology of place names, the quest becomes imaginative. I think about the Stone Age people who lived in the Severn vale, paddling their canoes along narrow strips of water between the reeds, hunting for geese, making homes out of reed and willow. I've paddled a canoe in one of the few watery places remaining, and I imagine this tells me something. I've walked between the river and the hills. I imagine the ancestors down by the river in the summer, but also using the woods for fuel and building materials. I know some of my ancestors of place buried some of their dead up on the hilltops, overlooking the plain and the river. There is speculation in my vision, but none the less I hold a keen sense of their presence, and the way in which their bodies have literally become the earth.

I find the imaginations of others of great assistance when it comes to ancestors of place. Not least in this are the artistic representations created by illustrators for books, museums and notice boards. Depictions of ordinary people, as they might have looked and lived, in whatever place I am in, are things I always find evocative. Going further than this, there are some places that now offer costumed waxworks as part of their exhibits – Warwick castle, for example, has figures of people who were known to have lived there, dressed appropriately for their period. The Jorvik centre in York includes people whose faces were reconstructed using a mix of art and science, working from bones in graveyards. We can't always know if we are indeed gazing upon the ancestors when we see these reconstructions, but they are powerful. There are paintings going back a fair way that give us some depiction of what the rich and important people of the day looked like. Some artists do chronicle peasant life as well, although there's far less of that. We learn a lot about costume from these images. Most people lived without having their face recorded. Bones can be the basis of viable reconstructions, using the same sorts of techniques that help identify the more recently dead. Bones can be refleshed, as we bring what we know to these ancestral remnants, and put a face on the past.

How we use and understand the bones of our ancestors is an issue I will return to later. From the simple perspective of connecting with our ancestors, having a face is invaluable. Names, dates and numbers are difficult to relate to, but when we depict the ancestors, they come alive to us.

Ancestors in the land

The land we walk on is made from the bodies of our ancestors of place. All things that die and return to the soil go to make up the fertile part of it. We live on the remains of the dead. Everything that we grow for food depends on the fertility of the soil. By this means the ancestors are also with us in everything we eat. We ingest them, and what was once part of them, becomes a part of us.

While human bodies have been returning to the soil for as long as there have been humans, this is another point at which we must acknowledge our non-human ancestry. The plants and creatures whose leaves and flesh have long since rotted down are equally our ancestors of place.

All that currently lives is made up of atoms that were once part of other bodies. It is not only our ancestors of blood who have a presence within our skin, but those of place as well.

Go back a few generations and people sourced their food far more locally. The ancestors who fed us were much more immediate, much more part of our place. Now that our food travels around the world, we are not so dependent on local production. This exposes us to far more bacteria, and weakens our connection to the ground we walk upon. Sourcing locally can rebuild that sense of connection, but that's not always possible, especially in urban environments. Perhaps instead it is better to consider the implications of eating the whole world. All of the ancestors of place are becoming the ancestors of our meals. We depend upon them all, and they too are entering into our bodies. If we are what we eat, that has physical as well as spiritual implications.

The earth is not only our mother. The soil is our grandmothers, our grandfathers. Grave, womb and table are all as one. Life feeds upon death. Each time we eat, we are engaging with a process that has been in existence since complex life on earth began. Our bodies are made out of history, full of tiny fragments that have been through all the ages humanity has known. We are made of trees and flowers, insects, mammals, fish. To some degree my body must contain fragments of human ancestors too. In time our flesh will be returned to this great cycle, to become part of something else. Does consciousness travel in tiny ways with the physical? Is awareness the consequence of many minuscule expressions of spirit, or life coming together in one form? I don't know. If it is so, then all that lives and all that lies in the soil embodies all that has ever been. If spirit lies in the atoms that make up our cells, then the spirit of our ancestors is alive and within us.

Living with ancestral legacies

When it comes to our own immediate environment, the legacies left by our ancestors of place are not always good. While it's tempting to think of beautiful half-timbered houses, castles, stone circles and other, equally romantic remnants, most manifestations of ancestors of place are more recent.

I spent a while visiting Birmingham, in the centre of the UK. It had been full of slum building, where families would live in a couple of rooms and share an outside toilet with a number of other houses. There were no baths in those dwellings. Most of these structures have gone, although a few were kept as a museum piece. To clear the slums, blocks of flats went up, and a small nearby market town – Redditch – was radically redeveloped. Coming into this area, my ancestors of place had left me, and everyone else, with cheap and nasty, low quality buildings, ugly sixties constructions, inadequate housing, and a sizeable population that had been dispossessed in the previous generation. The legacy of low aspiration and poor conditions continues.

I heard stories of the animal markets and abattoirs that had once existed in Birmingham, now replaced by shiny shopping centers alongside the concrete monstrosities. Redditch had vast areas entirely devoid of beauty. Row after row of identical houses in rabbit warren constructions, with people crammed in and few facilities to support them. Some of Birmingham was beautiful in terms of architecture but I remember clearly my first trip into the city on a train. The line took us through the now-demolished Longbridge plant, an old car factory. It was such a sad, ugly, grim sort of place. Coming to it from the serene Cotswolds made me want to cry. With time, I became accustomed to the sight, but it never stopped making me wince.

Sometimes the remnants of industry have a certain gothic splendor, or are elegant in decay. The docks around Gloucester were in serious disrepair for most of my childhood, but retained a definite charm. The ruins of once fine buildings – like the remains of city walls in York or Chester – remain appealing while decaying modern buildings are an eyesore. Our modern ancestors did not think about either beauty or longevity in their building designs, and we live with that.

Our recent ancestors also bequeath us, and many generations to come, with a legacy of nuclear waste. We had no say in this, just as our own descendants get no opportunity to protest over what we leave for them. The other forms of waste and pollution present in our environment could have all kinds of effects we know nothing about. As we use up the fossil fuels, deplete the fishing stocks and continue the legacy of industrial waste and environmental damage, we carry forward so many of the things our ancestors set in motion.

Just because we have embarked in a certain direction, does not make us obliged or fated to continue. We might imagine that 'progress cannot be stopped' we might think there is a moral imperative to do everything that we want to do. We would be wrong in this. Just as we do not have to perpetuate the behaviors and beliefs of others, so too are we not required to continue raping and pillaging our planet in the way our ancestors have done. We can choose to live differently. We can reject the legacy of consumerism, capitalism and the doctrine that market forces will solve everything. We can stop imagining that some future science innovation will mop up after us and start leaving a bit less mess in the first place. We have the potential to be the generation that says 'enough' and rejects all that is unsustainable and dishonorable in the legacy of our ancestors. We need not build any more slums, or push any more species to the point of extinction. We are not obliged to pollute, or to make this planet uninhabitable. Just because our recent ancestors broke their relationship with the earth, does not mean it will remain broken. We have the power to choose.

Druid ancestors of place

Aside from the relatively recent stone circles built by revivalists in the Welsh Gorsedd tradition, the UK does not sport any sites that are known to be both ancient and Druidic. From Aubrey's realization that Avebury was an ancient stone circle onwards, it has been popular to associate ancient Druids with the ancient stone circles of the British Isles. The trouble is, there isn't any evidence to support this. The Druids of historical texts are associated with the Iron Age and the tribes generally referred to as The Celts. The stone circles all pre-date the Iron Age.

Recent usage has created a link, in the public consciousness and that of many modern pagans, between ancient sites and Druids. This occurs most iconicly with Stonehenge, and to a lesser extent with Avebury, but modern Druids do love working in stone circles and other sites often see a Druid presence too. The image of a subset of modern Druids, with their pristine white robes would connect automatically in many minds with Stonehenge.

The question of whether ancient Druidry has any connection with these historical sites is beyond me to tackle. It depends in part on whether you assume Iron Age British culture to be a new thing, or whether, as the British Museum Press puts it, 'British Iron Age societies grew primarily from local, Bronze Age roots.'[44] Any modern claim to these sites based on ancient usage is always going to be contentious.

What this leaves us with generally in the UK is a shortage of any features in the landscape that can be ascribed to the Druids of old. If the classical texts are to be believed, ancient Druids worshipped in sacred groves, which of course are long gone. Groves of trees can easily be adopted as suitable places to gather, and potentially the sort of thing our ancestors would have used. But they aren't the actual sites.

Many Druids, of course, do not live in the UK, or in the areas of northern Europe that had a Celtic presence, and may also have had Druids. For many modern Druids therefore, there can be no historical Druidic presence in the landscape. As previously discussed in this chapter, there are many issues around simply appropriating whatever ancient sites are present. For most of us therefore, the ancient Druids are not available to us specifically as ancestors of place, although we may well be able to identify other appealing religious figures who are connected to our landscape.

Modern Druidry generally builds no temples and erects no stone circles. There is nothing discernible to show where most Druid groves gather to celebrate. A hundred years from now, our descendants of tradition (assuming we have any!) will not be able to confidently claim us as ancestors of place either. Perhaps this is as well. Sites like Stonehenge cause a great deal of controversy and difficulty. They have been a focus for conflict and clashes both physical and legal with authority. If a site is iconic, it draws attention. Many well-meaning individuals will be attracted to working there, perhaps more than the site can support. A subset of people will invariably want the kudos of being associated with it, and the authority they imagine controlling access to the site may give them. Ownership of place, as previously commented, all too easily becomes an exercise in power and control entirely at odds with any kind of spiritual life.

It is better to think of our Druidic ancestors of place as being everywhere. Picture them celebrating in nature, and leaving no trace behind. In Israel, over the centuries, far, far too many people have died for the dream of claiming the holy land. If there are no Druid ancestors of place, if there are no defined sacred places we can never come into conflict with each other over them. I think it is as well for us that the ancient Druids have not bequeathed us many specific sites to obsess and squabble over. As a tradition, I think that's one we should most certainly uphold. Our descendants should also benefit from the freedom to find their own sacred places, and to make their temples fleetingly out of a circle of likeminded people, and leave no trace behind when their work is done.

Chapter Eight

Ancestors of Tradition

The ancestors of tradition are, to a certain degree, people we have chosen for ourselves. Tradition is very much about the history of human action, so this set is usually people, and very unlikely to be plants or creatures.

Every field of human endeavor has its ancestors, unless you are in the unusual position of creating an entirely new area of activity. Even then, previous people active in related fields still hold the position of ancestors. The first men to walk on the moon had no ancestors of moon walking tradition, but undoubtedly belong to a long tradition of adventurers and explorers, for example.

Most of this chapter will focus on Druidic ancestors of tradition. However, before I plunge into those murky waters, I'd like to briefly explore the wider ancestry of modern Druids. We might want to consider the families and clans we craft from intention and fellow feeling, and how those relate to the influences of blood ties. Certain gatherings and communities in our lives create a profound sense of belonging, a heart-home that we turn to for solace, companionship and inspiration. In choosing our ancestors of tradition, and our living comrades, we are engaged in a process of deliberately recreating ourselves. Blood and place may have been decided for us by the accident of birth, but tradition is ours to do with as we will.

Each of us has come to Druidry by our own route, and will work more deeply with some aspects of it than others. I'm fascinated by philosophy, which means I have looked to modern pagan philosophers like Brendan Myers and Emma Restall Orr for ideas. I've nosed around in the wider field of philosophy, but not found any tradition there I felt enough at home with to try to explore in depth. My single biggest influence in this regard has been authors like Jostien Gaarder and Robert Pirsig, the author of Zen and the Art of Motorcycle Maintenance, along with all the others who play out philosophical themes in their work, rather than more formal philosophy.

Druidry as a spiritual path does not exist as a separate thing from the rest of life experience. Druids are also people who work, create, act politically, and so forth. In all of these aspects of our lives we have ancestors of tradition. When we are working in consciously Druidic ways, we might want to honor the non-Druidic ancestors whose work has, none the less, helped to shape our own Druidry.

It's important to hold clear boundaries here and to recognize that just because I consider a person to be an ancestor of tradition, does not mean they would like or approve of what I do. It's very easy to look at historical figures who inspire us and co-opt them retrospectively into The Druid Way. This is neither respectful nor honest but some of our more recent Druid ancestors have done so extensively. It is good to recognize fellow travelers and to acknowledge those who inspire us. It doesn't make them Druids. Oliver Rackham's writing on trees, and the human relationship with the countryside has significantly shaped my own understanding of this relationship. He has massively influenced how I perceive the use of land and resources, how I understand the place of humans in the wider picture, and how I consequently feel humanity should behave. This does not make him a Druid. I have no idea what his beliefs are, nor have I any right to make any assertions about him.

The ideas that modern Druidry depends on have a long tradition, and have been through all kinds of hands. The inspiration of Blake, the sensual celebration of the Pre-Raphaelites and their Arthurian imagery, the radical ideas of the Transcendentalists and many others have carried forward lines of thought that feed into the makings of modern Druidry. We would be deluding ourselves if we imagined that any of these forebears were consciously Druidic.

Sometimes it is tempting to see the essence of Druidry as a thing that exists in its own right, independent from any human minds that might contain it. If Druidry exists in this way, as a spiritual force, then of course its influence could be felt by many down the centuries who would not know to call themselves 'Druids'. It's a rather pleasing idea, and not provable in any rational way.

We might more productively think about the essential qualities of Druidry – inspiration, service, compassion, respect and responsibility to name some of the more obvious features. These are not ideas that are unique to us, nor are the ways in which we manifest them entirely original. A person who believed in the progress narrative might decide that humanity as a whole is steadfastly moving towards these values, and see Druidry as one manifestation of this. We might see the values underpinning Druidry as themselves being the spiritual goal of humanity.

How we understand the story of our spiritual evolution depends on which bits we choose to focus on. Druidry has not, in the past few hundred years, been an entirely glorious example of all that is best about humanity. Like every other human endeavor, it has been affected by politics, by the attention hungry, the power hungry and those whose relationship with reality may have been severely challenged. New generations of Druids bring new figures and voices to the mix, and a continual process of selecting and rejecting aspects of our history.

The stories we make about the history of Druids, and ancient Druidry, are also the stories we make about who we imagine ourselves to be and where we think this tradition is going. There isn't a great deal of factual certainty to be had. All of the comments that I've already raised around racial and cultural identity can also be applied to religious identity. It is a construct, made selectively and for a specific purpose. The legends of the spiritual tribe are no less divisive and able to cause bloodshed than the stories of nationhood and race. Part of religious identity functions to satisfy the human need to belong. Holding that identity without alienating, rejecting or devaluing others is not easy. Yet the call to responsibility, compassion and honor inherent in Druidry seems to me to demand just that.

This chapter is less about the hard facts of Druid history, more about the ways in which we latch on to bits of the available narratives, and places where perhaps we need to rethink our relationship with the past. I want to explore how we imagine our Druid ancestors, how it serves us to construct them in certain ways, and why there has been so much creative reconstruction. A hundred years ago the Druids of the time were reconstructing ancient Druidry as wearing the white nighty robes and donning fake beards. A significant percentage of today's Druids would reject the costumes for both themselves and their ancient ancestors. We might instead wear the kinds of slinky velvets favored by some wiccans. Our tastes might take us towards historical re-enactment style gear, or equally in the direction of walking boots and a sturdy coat. Let's pause and play with that.

Druid costume story number one
Obviously our ancient Druid ancestors would have dressed in practical ways for the conditions, using the best resources available to them at the time. We best re-create what they do by emulating that underlying idea rather than going for the historical costume.

Druid costume story number two
Obviously our Druid ancestors would have gone to great lengths to express beauty in their attire and to honor the gods through care of their own appearance. We know the Celts were serious about their torcs and attire. Our Druid ancestors would have

worn the best and most attractive clothing available to them at the time. Therefore we should wear the best that we can find by modern standards, because the ancient Druids wouldn't have been trying to hark back to the sort of gear Stone Age people wore, would they?

Druid costume story number three

Obviously our Druid ancestors' appearance would have been influenced by being out in the wilds so much. Maybe they wore feathers in their hair, and wore animal skins to show their affiliation with certain spirits. The most authentic Druid look has the 'through a hedge backwards' element to it, and may include bare skin or full on nudity.

I could go on like this indefinitely, building models for modern dress out of stories. It serves to illustrate a point. We do not live in the same conditions our Druidic ancestors knew. If we did know exactly what they did, wore, said and the like, at least some of it would make no sense in a modern context. If we seek for the underlying reasoning for aspects of ancient Druidry (or how we imagine ancient Druidry) we will inevitably impose our own understanding upon that, bring our own values to it and interpret it in our own terms. The best we can hope to do this way is justify ourselves with reference to the past. I think it makes more sense to focus instead on exploring our own motives and reasoning to better understand ourselves, with an aim to working with that.

However, all of us to some degree carry a story about our spiritual ancestors of tradition. We have a narrative about them that gives us context, and possibly shapes our spiritual journey. Some of this story may have been passed on or acquired from dubious sources. An element of the story very likely comes from our own wishes or aspirations. If we carry these tales without exploring them, we are shaped by stories without necessarily understanding how that works. We may inherit things that, if we knew their origins we would feel obliged to reject. We may also be carrying under-explored ideas that encourage us in beliefs that are dysfunctional, counter-productive or misguiding us. When we take a story, any story, for granted, we give it free access to our unconscious where it can influence us. Every time we question a story and engage with it, we take conscious control over its place within our lives.

Druidry as a tradition is very much about deliberate choice, active responsibility and the reasoned use of inspiration for the good of all. Allowing yourself to be unconsciously shaped by someone else's story simply does not fit in with this philosophy. This is why I feel it is so important to scrutinize the stories we have about Druid ancestry, and to take collective control of our own stories to better understand ourselves and to make more conscious choices about how we take our spiritual path forwards.

The ancient Druids and other early pagans

One of the problems facing contemporary pagans is the story about our ancestors. It is a widely held belief that ancient pagans were an unwashed, uncivilized, barbarous lot practicing human sacrifice, horribly superstitious and in the sway of a manipulative priesthood. This story has an ongoing use for a subset of the population. It reinforces the idea that paganism was bad and that the rise of Christianity represented progress. In this story, ideas about ancient pagans are simplified – focusing on war, squalor, and superstition. The arts, philosophies, explorations, agricultural skills, laws and other social complexities of our ancestors' lives are simply swept under the carpet. We can see this story at play in film and fiction from asides in Thomas Hardy's Tess of the D'Urbervilles through to The Wicker Man and beyond. It serves an agenda that seeks to devalue non-industrial living.

Taught history in Britain tends to begin with the Romans and largely focuses on life after the Norman Conquest. When I went through school the Celts weren't even mentioned. Before the Romans, my earliest impression was of Stone Age figures. It was some time before I had opportunity to fill in those gaps for myself, but far more people will not have done. And thus the vague uncertainties of ancient history are perpetrated through lack of education. The Christian narrative that pre-Christians were a misguided lot who needed saving, is pervasive and often goes unchallenged. Talking with a friend of my son's recently, I discovered this boy assumed that being a modern Druid still meant human sacrifice. He's an intelligent, well-read child, and has absorbed what for a long time was the 'normal' understanding of paganism.

Inspired by lurid films and gothic horror imagery, many people have a narrative of both ancient and modern pagans as being people who sacrifice virgins, indulge in orgies and dance naked in the woods. I've lost count of how many people, when first hearing that I'm pagan, have asked about the virgins, and the naked dancing. Often the questions are half in jest, because folk are increasingly aware that it just doesn't add up properly, but they have no idea what an alternative narrative might be.

The stories everyone 'knows' about ancient pagans owe a lot to Roman writers, who many of us now feel had a lot of reasons to be less than perfectly accurate. However, bits of those 'classic' texts have been taught in schools and published in books for generations, supporting the Christian version in which all pre-Christians were barbarous, and feeding into colonial ideas about superiority over superstitious, native peoples. There have been a great many reasons, culturally, for maintaining the story that pagans were, and therefore are, dangerous and unpleasant. (I mentioned at the beginning of the book to be wary of authors who make vague allusions to classical authors. I'd like to acknowledge here that the only classical-author-stories in my head are those vague ones, and the vague but widespread use of them is more my point here than any exact content.)

The story modern pagans have about ancient pagans is totally at odds with this. The fiction we write about ourselves – The Apple and The Thorn by Walter William Melnyk and Emma Restall Orr, and Walter William Melnyk's Marsh Tales, being prime examples – construct historical pagans in a completely different way. In our versions of the story, ancient pagans are more usually gentle, enlightened people, living close to nature, and reverencing gods of the land. They are keepers of wisdom. The priests and Druids in their populous always have a huge knowledge of herbal healing. Quite often in this kind of fiction, the magic works. We draw on stories recorded in Wales and Ireland in mediaeval times, on what we can glean from archaeology, and from the desire to re-cast our ancestors as a much nicer bunch.

There are a number of pagan friendly fictions coming through now whose authors' own beliefs I know little about. That they aren't marketing themselves as pagans (to my knowledge) but are offering pagan-friendly narratives suggests to me that the story of wicked ancient paganism is no longer in the ascendant. We live in more tolerant times, and our relationship with indigenous people in other countries, and other belief systems, have complicated the context in which society as a whole thinks about ancient paganism. If it thinks about it at all.

At college I encountered post-colonial fiction and magical realism. There are concepts here I think have huge potential for modern paganism, but that don't seem to be permeating through. Here's a crash course. Post-colonial fiction comes from countries that were colonized by European countries, and are now reclaiming their cultures. European colonialism was not merely a taking of land, it included forcing Christianity onto indigenous people, and forcing a European language onto the colonized. Colonialism brought the tradition of western rationalism to cultures that had previously been guided by their own, unique world view. Post-colonial fiction reclaims these repressed traditions and beliefs, as best it can.

Magical realism takes many forms based on a world view that is not underpinned by western rationalism. It gives different ways of knowing and being, rooted in traditional cultures and is part of a kind of identity that colonialism sought to wipe out. Thus the magical elements are often critically important in post-colonial fiction. This kind of writing counts as 'serious literature' – it's the genre Salman Rushdie belongs to, along with Isabel Allende, and Toni Morrison.

When white, western people write fiction about magic, it falls into the genre of fantasy. It might be paranormal or urban fantasy, but it's generally deemed to be low-brow genre fiction and not to be taken seriously. Our own traditional cultures, the folk traditions that still exist, and the ways of perceiving the world that are intuitive rather than empirical are there to be reclaimed and reinvented. If magical realism is a viable expression in countries emerging from the legacy of colonialism, then it is a viable genre anywhere. It is possible to tell stories about life experience that are neither irrelevant fantasy, nor defined by the profoundly non-magical worldview dominating the mainstream.

While the majority of pagan people are, in my experience, very creative folk, not all are makers of stories for sale. Whether we write stories for others or not, we all have a narrative sense of our ancient pagan ancestors. The stories we tell to ourselves are the most important ones. Having a strong framework in which to hold a magical-realism story about paganism, has a lot of potential. There are other ways of seeing the world. Science-based understanding is not the only one of value. Science will not tell you what makes a painting good, and it won't tell you where ideas come from. Economic based narratives of living will not actually tell you much about value. Political stories about the best kinds of society will not inform you how best to live as an individual. As pagans, we have to construct our own narrative.

When we think about the ancient Druids, there's far too little hard, historical fact to construct any sound academic version of what they did and how they did it. Thinkers like Graeme Talboys and Brendan Myers have done great work reconstructing the worldviews and philosophies of our pagan ancestors, especially the Celts, but the odds are there will always be more questions than answers. I recommend reading as much history as you can, as you set out to build your understanding of the past. If nothing else, it gives you something firm to wield when dealing with people from a more empirical background.

Here's another difficulty Druids face:

It seems clear at least that the Britons had no common pantheons of deities with defined powers, but myriad deities of the tribe, and of places.

Whilst it is true that there were recognizably similar forms of burial practice, ritual behavior, settlement layouts, distinctive art styles, a group of closely related languages, common mythical themes, and similar social structures across a wide geographical area, this does not mean the Celts were a homogenous group. There were wide variations through time as the culture evolved in response to internal and external pressures. There were also wide variations from place to place. It is the language and common cultural practices that bound these peoples together.[45]

In short, there is no one single 'historical Druidry'. Druidry is identifiably specific to location and time, with variations across locations and times. There is no one single thing we can uncover, no one, authentic form that constitutes ancient Druidry.

The most solid historical insights give us far more questions than answers. There is so much room, between the lines, to shoehorn in almost anything we like. Which doesn't mean we should, of course.

Early reconstructionists viewed the ancient Druids as being

male, hierarchical, and patriarchal – very much in line with the ethos of their own time. The advent of female Druids as any kind of presence is a twentieth century feature by the looks of it, and the arrival of female leaders within the community belongs to the late twentieth century onwards. This is consistent with wider social norms. These days, women hold positions of power, and therefore our imagining of ancient Druids can now also include the idea that women held positions of power then too. As society becomes more questioning of power structures, so modern Druidry moves away from hierarchy towards greater equality, with anarchic groups connecting with each other in creative ways. This too can be imagined into the past.

When we look at history, we are often searching for our own reflection. There's a BBC Radio program called The Long View – where the underlying premise is to take a modern issue and find a historical point of comparison and see what can be learned by contrasting them. Most of us do not explore history for its own sake, but for what it can teach us about where we are, how we got here, and how we might proceed. We look to the past for validation, and for contact with something that feels like us. In just the same way when we imagine the distant future, we people it with humanoid aliens whose world views, emotions and cultures are perfectly comprehensible to us. Anything not so human will likely be cast as the villain.

I would recommend sitting down with your ideas about ancient Druids, or ancient pagans more generally, and trying to pin down the story you have. If you can, ascertain where elements in it have come from. There are no right answers here. Stories sourced in art and fiction are just as valid, in this assessment, as stories rooted in archaeology or classical texts. The important thing is to know what your story is, and to have some idea where you got it from. Pay special attention to those elements you cannot locate a source for, they will very likely be the most ingrained, the most certainly held and the ones most in need of scrutiny.

Once you have clarity about your vision of the past, ask what purpose this serves in your life. What do you gain from this take on history? What ideas does it reinforce? What does it enable you to reject or disregard? How does it hold up a mirror to your own life and to what extent is it to do with your aspirations for the future?

Sometimes, going deeply into the story brings to light ideas and beliefs that are not as helpful to us as we might have assumed. Examining the story can reveal aspects taken from hostile sources, reactions to the dominant culture, and other elements that once conscious of them, we may deliberately reject. We might also find embarrassingly fluffy and romantic desires underpinning our historical narrative, and might want to amend those. Taking control of the story, we can decide what it is for, how we want to work with it, and we can develop a story that helps us feel centered and inspired. Going through this exercise also establishes very clearly that we are indeed working in the realms of story, not hard fact. The sharing of such stories can be powerful, but when they are given honestly as stories, not as empirical truth, we become more honest with ourselves and in many ways better equipped to deal with people whose world views do not match ours.

I began consciously working with my own narratives in my late teens. Growing up in a green and loosely pagan household, I had taken onboard a number of assumptions: Science is bad and makes things worse. The past was better. Society is heading in the wrong direction. By my late teens I had constructed an idea of how I wanted the world to be – pastoral, rural, arty, feminist. For a while I believed the narrative about ancient matrilineal goddess worshipping societies that existed before men took control. I liked the sound of that. Being a writer, I started playing out my ideas in fiction, and went on to write an atrocious and clichéd dystopian science fiction novel. I'm glad to say no copies of it remain in existence. Having written it, I realized that is was profoundly wrong. I hated the world I had constructed – it was oppressive, it limited creativity by rejecting certain lines of thought. The world view I wanted to promote, when it came to playing it out, sucked.

I might feel more uncomfortable about this personal story had I not then spent a chunk of my late teens exploring communism. On paper, it's a beautiful system. The only trouble is, it doesn't actually work, as twentieth century history illustrates only too well. What we imagine will go very nicely and what works in practice don't always equate. Not least because humans are a varied, unpredictable bunch.

In my years as an editor and reviewer, I've read a fair few pieces of fiction from folks with their own ideas of Utopia, and I've yet to read one that convinced me. The more effort we put into making it lovely according to our own values, the greater a chance, I am inclined to think, that it would be vile in practice. As soon as we have to enforce the loveliness from the top down, we are doomed to create tyrannies. Only that which comes up from the ground level, rooted and real, has a chance of flowering into something good and non-oppressive. I like to think of this as a 'bottoms-up' philosophy, with all due silliness and innuendo.

This matters because our ideas of 'best' inform the choices we make. The dreams we build about our ancient pagan ancestors shape our actions. The stories we tell about the past, the stories we tell to ourselves in quiet moments, are the stories informing how we think we want things to be. It's painfully easy to get that wrong, as I hope my own story illustrates. At least all I was doing was writing a novel no one would ever read. I wasn't setting out on a political career, or raising an army.

I am fascinated by revolutions, although I'm no expert in the history of them. My impression is that at the outset, there is invariably a rush of hope and enthusiasm, a belief in the scope to bring about a better world. It's all going to be brilliant. Often in revolutions the ends are assumed to justify the means and that's often a part of the problem. Many revolutions don't work and instead make things worse, as the ideals that started them mutate out of all recognition. My teenage rural idyll, my forced return to the past is not a million miles from the ideology of extremists like the Taliban. Looking back, that horrifies me. How many other people, driven by misguided, romantic ideology and a vision of something better, have contributed to creating something insane, totalitarian or otherwise destructive?

Even if we don't find ourselves caught up in a revolution, we need to get our stories straight. The wrong story will soothe and support us as we wander towards our own destruction.

Frauds and re-inventors

In terms of shaping the form of modern Druidry, the early recon-structionists have had considerable influence. The words 'gorsedd' and 'awen' come to us from them – or more specifically Iolo Morganwg. I've been told that the term 'Druidry' may have been coined even more recently by Ross Nichols. I get the impression 'Druid' is not the Celtic word, but one we get from the Romans, while Celt may come from the Greek Keltoi. Everything we have has been made up by someone.

When I first started attending Druid rituals, I had no idea how old any of the content was or who had come up with it. I assume this will be true of most people commencing a study of Druidry. Much of our ritual content, our commonly used prayers, even the structures favored by orders owe more to figures from the begin-nings of reconstruction than they do to antiquity. The trouble is that many of these people, but Iolo Morganwg most especially, were in the business of fabricating the past. We have a recent tradition in which well intentioned subsequent work has then been undertaken by people drawing on fabrications, and delib-erate frauds.

Alongside this we have the ancestors of tradition who meant

well, but were later proved wrong – Aubrey with his interpretations of Avebury as Druidic would be an obvious example. There
are the various artists, writers and politicians who reinvented the
Celtic identity as part of nation building in Ireland, Wales,
Scotland and France. The political aims are arguably good, but
the appropriation of history is, as always, problematic for
anyone looking back at it. There were people working with translations, or in second languages where their grasp may have been
tenuous. There's also been a selection process around what gets
translated in the first place.

Sometimes we can see giants standing on the shoulders of far
lesser creators, their own genius hampered by the way in which
drawing on inadequate research has informed their own output.
Here I'm inclined to think of the colossal influence Frazer's
Golden Bough appears to have had on Robert Graves – having
read them in quick succession about a decade ago, I felt sure that
Graves had been inspired in part by Frazer. The poetic qualities
of Graves' work still stand, but the faulty thinking underpinning
Frazer's anthropology remains a problem. The work of Graves
can then be seen going on to influence modern Druid groups.
Druidry has more than its share of high quality and well intentioned work underpinned by problematic sources and
questionable interpretations.

The wider pagan community has so many comparable issues
to face. Thinkers who become discredited in academic fields
continue to be read, and believed, by pagan authors operating
outside academic circles. We are telling new stories, built on the
foundation of older stories, without always knowing who came
up with those stories and why. It is all too easy to create an
impression of knowledge and certainty. Quote an impressive
sounding published source, throw in the correctly laid out
footnotes, write in a confident, third person way that makes you
sound like a serious commentator, and how is someone new to
paganism or unfamiliar with your field going to know? A trained

academic interested in your specific area might spot the failings, but a regular reader might not. Over the years I have seen so many articles where I really wasn't sure about the accuracy, proffering speculations as hard fact, or spinning ideas into improbable explanations.

Perhaps one of the simplest examples of this is the ley line theory. The gist of it is that there are earth energy lines connecting sacred sites, and these lines themselves have a special power. Again in my distant teens I took an interest in this issue. Take a map, draw a line on it connecting sites – churches, old burial sites, anything of passable antiquity will do. There's never been any requirement to draw only from one period. Lo and behold, straight lines appear, and in places they cross over each other. I've heard pagans at moots talking about ley lines as if they were unassailable fact. Experiences will be explained in terms of them. You can throw ley lines at any topic, sacred geometry as well for that matter, with the confidence that they can be made to stick, and that few questions will be asked. These are stories that have been told so often that we don't even need to explain were we got them from. We just take them for granted as part of our truth, our world view, and on we go.

This returns me to the issue of knowing where a thing comes from. Would you feel the same way about a prayer if you knew it had been written by a man who went on to pass it off as ancient religion, for his own gain? Would any of his words about truth and integrity sit well, with that knowledge in mind? This is precisely the issue I find myself wrangling with when it comes to Iolo Morganwg and his influence on modern Druidry. He made it up. That in itself is less of an issue for me than the fact that he made it up and then tried to pretend it was much older. The intellectual fraud implicit in this is entirely at odds with honor and integrity.

There's many a pagan figure who has claimed knowledge from secret sources, mysterious teachers, ancestors now departed, writings copied and passed down from centuries ago. Gerald Gardner claimed not to have invented Wicca, and there seems to be uncertainty still about whether he did or not. In wider spiritual life, people have been claiming as much and more for their texts ever since religions were first written down, by the look of it. Other religions' books are channeled from divine sources. All of the book religions rely on the idea of their books being the word of God. Groups like the Mormons depend on the idea that their leaders had personal revelations to guide humanity. Spiritualists of all kinds will claim spirit guides, teachers in the inner realms, on the ether, memories from past lives, from Akashic records, the collective unconscious or wherever else you want to place your inspiration.

There's a common theme here worth examining in more detail. It is that spiritual people across time and culture have been very nervous about claiming their spiritual inspiration as their own. Perhaps we all assume we will be taken more seriously if ours is the literal word of God, or the spell book passed down by our grandmothers. We fall back on the idea that antiquity equates to validity, which is not necessarily true. Old ideas can be just as wrong as new ones, with all due reference to flat earth theories and intelligent design.

Iolo Morganwg was a brilliant man. He had an amazing vision of peace and human harmony, of cultural expression and identity that has actually benefitted Wales in the form of its poetic assemblies. He did not publish that inspiration as his own. I've heard plenty of Druids voice the argument that in the climate of the times, he could not have done, and that only by attaching his vision to antiquity could he get it in front of other people. This may be so. Do the ends justify the means? Is the brilliance of the man in any way reduced by the lengths he went to, to share his words?

There are many figures in the history of spirituality who have more in common with Morganwg than not. In fields of philosophy and politics, people are entirely at ease claiming their ideas as their own. While due reference may be made to human sources of inspiration, we don't hear many inventors claiming divine influence, or many politicians explaining that their ideas come from the wisdom of enlightened beings who live in the clouds. It's fine to claim religion as a politician, but not that you specifically are the recipient of divine inspiration. That invites ridicule.

The stories we have about spirituality are very different from those we build about other aspects of human existence. Perhaps the closest area of overlap is between religion and creativity. Artists and authors are routinely asked where they get their ideas from – a question that presupposes an external answer. If we all thought that inspiration comes from 'inside your head' no one would bother to ask about the source. The invention of an even faster car is a rational, logical thing and we expect the sources of inspiration to be appropriately prosaic. The creation of a poem, an opera, or a spiritual creed is something else entirely. We see it as inherently irrational and so to validate it, we get God in on the process.

I've been making things up for as long as I can remember. Life has brought me into contact with creative people working in all kinds of fields. The problem with all 'art' is that people on the outside of it see only the finished piece. They imagine some wild burst of creative frenzy, during which the ideas blaze through the artist and out into the world. In practice, it is never like this. Lots of mundane things have to happen along the way. It would be like hearing a tune played on a violin, and ascribing the sound being emitted to magic. To play a tune on a violin, someone has to first make the instrument out of wood, put strings on it and get them in tune. It is the same for any form of creativity. For the music of inspiration to play, the instrument, the creator, must first be ready.

All of human endeavor has the capacity to be creative. The

subjects we call 'arts' are in no way unique in this regard. Teaching is a tremendously creative profession, so is reconstructive surgery but who interviews either type of professional to see where their ideas come from? All creative work begins with learning. We learn about the tools and material involved. We learn about those who have already done great things in our field. We learn the habits, conventions, the history of the form, and we work on getting the technical skills together to be able to replicate what has gone before. For a while, we copy others, and then if we stick at it long enough to have a degree of mastery we start to do our own thing. It is as true for needlecraft as it is for materials science and recorder playing. Why should spiritual inspiration be any different?

Something inherent in the way we think about spirituality makes us want to source the inspiration elsewhere. Is this because we unconsciously assume that spirit also is somewhere else? The more we reject our own innate spirituality, the less inclined we are to see the god within, or the profundity of our own vision, and the more readily we source our ideas outside ourselves. It certainly doesn't help that we have a wider culture with thousands of years of external divine inspiration being cited as the source of human spirituality.

When we place revelation in the hands of a god, we give authority to the vision that is wholly independent of us. 'I have to do this because god told me' can make any action palatable, when compassionate humanity would reject it outright. One of the stories that has always horrified me from the Old Testament has God testing Abraham by demanding he sacrifice his son. I'd like to think that if a god went so far as to manifest in front of me and demand the same, I would tell them exactly where they could stick the idea. Better death than dishonor, and I can think of no greater betrayal than to take your child's life in the name of a god. To take anyone else's life for a deity, or to punish transgression of 'god's laws' with death seems reprehensible to me as well. But we construct the story in which god is external to us, transcendent if you will, the inspiration comes from *Him* and we are not responsible for it. We just have to obey. I should note that this story belongs to a time when human sacrifice may have been a lot more normal, and that does change things in terms of how I think about it in context.

What happens when we place the human inspiration for spiritual practice squarely within the human sphere? If we do this, every story about religion has to be judged in terms of what it achieves in the world, not by how it measures up to some inhuman notion of divine interference. I have a longstanding suspicion that all 'revelation' is inherently human, and that it's about time we started taking responsibility both for it, and its consequences.

How does this relate to the reconstructionist Druids? We might appear to have gone off at rather a dramatic tangent here, but there is a significant degree of relevance I think. Once we assume that spiritual revelation can only be in the head of the one experiencing it, we have to re-evaluate anyone who has claimed spiritual inspiration.

One of the things that can be said of all our creative, fraudulent ancestors in the Druid tradition, is that none of them, to my knowledge, claimed to be getting their inspiration directly from God. They offered work and insight as belonging to the wisdom of earlier people, and in some cases assumed a connection, admittedly, with those book traditions and ideas of original divine revelation. But they did not offer their own creativity as revelation, and I find that very interesting.

If inspiration is human, then where it came from – which human it came from and in what precise circumstances – matters less than how it moves us forward. If it resonates, if it makes sense and has the capacity to enrich, that has to be a far more important measure of worth than how far back it can be traced. We need to know as best we can where our ideas come from, and why they were brought into the world, but we need not reject anything that actually works for us.

I think this also has relevance when looking at the issues around mediaeval texts. I've not devoted a whole section to this issue precisely because I don't have enough usefully to say about it. The Mabinogian, the Tain, the poems ascribed to Taliesin, Amergin and others are beautiful, creative works. They represent a vibrant culture, and deep contemplation of them has much to offer a modern Druid. We don't know to what degree they are ancient and to what degree they were re-invented, or entirely created by mediaeval monks. Does it matter? Not if we can use them. We cannot claim authority based on them, but that's something I am increasingly passionate about anyway. We should not even be seeking that kind of 'authority'. We should be basing our spirituality in what works, what makes sense, not in the age or precise sourcing.

Fraternal Druidry

For some people, Druid ancestors are much more real, immediate and confusing. One of the questions most frequently directed to The Druid Network's Office, and to its Directory during my time there, went like this. 'I have just discovered that my grandfather was a Druid. I've got a photo of him in his robes, and have some kind of medal that belonged to him. Please can you tell me more about what he was doing?'

There's a rather charming set of assumptions underpinning such queries; that modern Druidry is essentially organized, could be expected to have records dating back a hundred years, and that the kind of Druidry the ubiquitous grandfather was doing in his robes will be the same as the kind of Druidry of an overtly spiritual organization like The Druid Network. None of these assumptions are accurate, and we directed people to the few surviving fraternal Druid orders in the hopes they might find out more there.

My story about fraternal Druidry is as follows. Once upon a time there were a bunch of people who desperately wanted to be Freemasons, but for whatever reason, could not get in. They decided to just go ahead and set up their own version of Freemasonry, resplendent with costumes, secret signs, quasi-mystical history and initiation rites that were not to be spoken of, and proceeded to gather for feasting, music, and later for charitable purposes and mutual aid. Some of them took to doing public rituals – heavy on the Christian influences and most of these organizations died the death when fraternal organizations generally became less relevant and popular in the first half of the twentieth century. Anyone who wants the actual historical story, which is far more complex and interesting, should read Ronald Hutton's Blood and Mistletoe.

My story version may sound a touch facetious, but there are a number of legacy issues from this period that I don't think serve modern Druidry at all. Firstly there's the hunger for titles, the infamous 'arch-Druid' comes from this sort of time – partly the fault of the fraternals, partly ascribable to the more spiritual reconstructionists. There were some significant overlaps so it's not entirely fair to treat them as two separate groups. The second issue is that as groups splintered, it all became a bit Monty Python. Speaking creatively, The Order of Druids begets an Ancient Order of Druids, a Really Ancient Order of Druids, an Even More Ancient Than Everyone Else Order of Druids, as folks created ever more elaborate and fictitious histories for themselves. Once again the issue of trying to create legitimacy by falsely claiming antiquity raises its ugly head.

There are going to be a significant number of people out there who have a recent ancestor who was a Druid. Experience of people for whom this is the case inclines me to think they understand this in terms of mystical Druidry, not gathering-in-the-back-room-of-a-pub-for-a-pint Druidry. Although as the modern moot demonstrates, there's not always much difference! People who do not consider themselves to be pagans nonetheless take delight in imagining their recent ancestors to have been involved in the movement.

For example, an elderly friend of mine considered his father to have been a pagan. His main evidence for this was that his father carried a rattly tin no one was allowed to touch and they thought he kept small bones in it. Alongside this, he had belonged to the Ancient Order of Foresters. The title sounds impressive, conjuring up a long tradition of men who are wise in the mysteries of ancient woodlands. Like so many other 'ancient' orders, it's fairly recent and was in his case probably some fraternal muster for men of significant local status. However, in family legend he will go down as a pagan, a Forester, and a figure of mystery and interest. Whether he was actually pagan, is unknowable.

Pagans are not the only people to delight in the witchy granny story. As we romanticize our blood ancestors and make good stories out of them, we may easily ascribe beliefs to them they did not have, and place them in traditions they were not actually a part of. Where membership of groups with obviously Druidic names are concerned, the ease of imagining something that never was, is almost irresistible.

For fraternal Druids, this issue of tradition and ancestry goes both ways. Most fraternal Druid groups are not spiritual, but no doubt get their share of queries from folk who want to be Druids in the mystical magical sense. The other non-spiritual Druid group, the Eisteddfods, also run into this issue. Everyone knows that Winston Churchill was a Druid, and that the current Archbishop of Canterbury is also a Druid. It's a word that means very different things in different settings, and here pertains to the recent tradition of Welsh poetry contests, in which people are titled as Druids, partly thanks to good old Iolo Morganwg's influence again. But these are not people who, in any spiritual sense, would consider themselves to be following a Druidic path

– it's simply a title associated with a cultural event.

Spiritual Druidry, Cultural Druidry and Fraternal Druidry are interconnected, share a common ancestry, a degree of common language, and in many people's minds are indistinguishable. From the perspective of the people involved, the differences are vast and very important, but from the outside, we are all Druids, all as likely to stick on the false beards, and all part of the same narrative about what eccentric people get up to in the spare time.

Christian Druids

One of the stories about ancient Druids that comes to us from the revivalists, is that they had a close relationship with Christianity. To recap this narrative, when humanity was young, divine revelation was given to all people. The Jews managed to hold a decent version of it together, but most civilizations fell into terrible pagan ways, worshipped idols, danced naked, sacrificed virgins… Now one of two things happens. Either the Druids also kept that original teaching alive, or it was later transmitted – in some versions directly by Abraham himself – to them. Either way, historical Druidry represented a very pure form of Christianity in which veneration for The One True God was very much at the heart of things.

Consequently, when Christian missionaries arrived in England, the Druids were quick to embrace the faith, recognizing it as the natural successor of their own – in some versions the one they had prophesized and waited for. English Christianity under the Druids then remained pure and untainted by the decadence of Rome.

There is a variation in which the Druids were wise people in their own right, had no prior exposure to Christianity or Judaism, but recognized its value anyway, and its growing social importance so opted to become Christian. In this version British Christianity retains much of the wisdom of the Druids, giving rise to a specifically Celtic Christianity.

This story, in either variant, is at odds with the narrative that pre-Christian pagans were an inferior lot who needed saving from themselves. However, it functions in a very specific way for English identity, establishing the uniquely English brand of Christianity as being far superior to anyone else's, a story with an appeal in certain quarters that is easy to spot.

If you accept the story that the Druids became Christians by this route, then early 'Celtic' Christian writing is the natural inheritor of ancient Druid wisdom, and could be an especially pure form of Christianity in its own right. That the Roman church sought to suppress it is, from a certain perspective, additional proof of it having value.

The stories that explicitly link Druidry with Christianity have a number of functions. Firstly, they claim the Druids as icons for Christians. Secondly, they validate an English, or Celtic, church – depending on your perspective and national identity. Thirdly, they fit into a narrative that emphasizes the similarities between faiths rather than the differences, and fourthly this set of stories allows people to very comfortably place themselves as Druid Christians, Christian Druids, Celtic Christians, or to blend the two faiths in other ways. There are a significant number of people doing just this, and so far as I can tell, they are equally perplexing to pagan Druids and other Christians. They do, however, offer an excellent illustration of the relationship between the stories we have and the things we choose to do. Without an underpinning story connecting the two positions, this alignment would be far harder to achieve.

Other Pagan/Christian crossovers tend to associate Mary with mother goddess figures, to associate Jesus with a Frazer-style sacrifice god, and/or to equate saints with pre-Christian deities. However, personal experience inclines me to believe that while plenty of pagans have no problem with Jesus and Mary as possible extra deities, folk actively mixing other pagan and Christian practice are relatively unusual compared to the numbers exploring the Celtic-Christian-Druid connections. It no doubt helps that this tradition has some texts to draw on and a degree of known history to refer to.

Many of the reconstructionist Druids who shaped modern Druidry where themselves Christian. Stukely was in fact a vicar, although this after the more overtly Druidic period of his life. In the early days of antiquarianism, many of the people involved were vicars. Fraternal Druidry was explicitly Christian, and drew on that tradition for its public musters. It wasn't about setting up any kind of alternative spiritual movement at all. The cultural Druids are sufficiently compatible with Christianity to count the Archbishop of Canterbury amongst their number.

Modern Druidry was born out of a largely Christian society. Evidence for folk magic[46] makes it clear that for many people, magical practice and Christianity went hand in hand, no trouble at all. Priests could bless stones and throw them into fields to make the crops grow. The Host, if appropriated from a church, could be used in spells. Charms and prayers are sometimes indistinguishable. 'Mathew, Mark, Luke and John, bless the bed that I lie on,' was one such example I learned as a child.

Whether we are thinking about what might, or might not have happened to Celtic culture and the Druids after the Romans had left, or our more recent ancestors, there is clearly scope for a complex narrative about the relationship between Christianity and Druidry. For people who come to paganism precisely because they are unhappy with their experience of Christianity, that can be an uncomfortable line of thought. I would imagine it would be equally unpalatable for anyone who sees Christianity as inherently superior and untarnished by pagan influences.

There are pagans who are very clear in their stories, and reject all connections between paganism and Christianity, save to claim that 'they' have taken a lot of material from 'us'. I think the story of overlap, of mutual borrowing and influence is a far more interesting one to consider. Not least because of the possibilities it gives us for the future.

I've spent the last year or so in a rural part of England. Here, the church-going population is both small, and aging. At the same time, villages have lost most of their amenities – pubs, schools, doctors, shops and other basic requirements have been stripped out in the last few decades, leaving communities with little of their own. The churches are sometimes the only communal focal point there is left. They are beautiful buildings, and woefully underused. I'm seeing how book lending schemes run through churches are offsetting the decline of library services. Churches become events venues, host art shows, local history exhibitions and conservation efforts.

As a Druid, I am not only interested in community, but drawn to give what service I can in my local community. Out here in the villages, that means working with the church – there's nowhere else to go. As I have started to put in an appearance at coffee mornings and other such events, at a number of different churches, I've seen the same pattern emerge. After a little conversation, I'll be invited to attend a service. I will explain that while I am very supportive of community, I don't do services. In the first round of conversation, the topic will then drop. The second, or perhaps third time a Christian group encounters me, someone will push a little further, and I will tell them I'm a Druid. At this point, the line, 'The church is for everyone, and you are very welcome to be here' follows.

In a church where most of the small community is over sixty, that I'm under forty, and present, and interested makes the minor detail of my not being a Christian really not worth fussing over. When I began poking around in local churches, I had never imagined such a response, but everywhere I've gone, it's been the same. When I lived in the Midlands, I found that our both being spiritual women, priestess to our tribe, gave me far more in common with the local vicar than the differences of faith did to divide us. We talked on an equal footing about some issues, and when it came to handling my first funeral, she was one of the people who supported me in understanding the work involved.

I have at points in this book pointed to specific aspects of Christianity that I have enormous trouble with. My issues are usually around what people do with their own stories. What we do in the name of a religion does not necessarily define said religion. My experience has been that honorable people of any faith tend to have more productive common ground than reason to argue. Dishonorable people, of any faith, will use the language of belief, quote from texts, or whatever other trappings their religion offers, to serve their own ends. For these reasons I would advocate embracing any honorable person of any faith community and being open to their ideas. The dishonorable uses religions are put to should not be used to invalidate the faith itself. There are, after all, people who use paganism to further an expressly fascist agenda.

My story about what religion is and does includes the idea that we could all get along with each other perfectly well. Intolerance and dishonor are far bigger issues undermining inter-faith relationships, than the name we give to our beliefs.

Modern ancestors

While for many faith groups, the most important ancestors of tradition are entirely historical figures, modern pagans and Druids especially are in the interesting position of living alongside the 'ancestors'. Druidry is a young enough faith that we may in fact be living with those who will later be seen as founders of the spiritual side of modern Druidry. A large percentage of our ancestors of tradition are long since departed, but being a faith in the process of continually reinventing itself, our most recent ancestors are very much alive, with us and available for comment. It's also possible that the nature of Druidry will mean that each generation of new ancestors will have an important role, and that our older ancestors will not become the definitive voice of the tradition.

Every long-lived faith group has its ongoing supply of re-inventors, leaders and interpreters, so that to a certain degree any spiritual person will have living ancestors of tradition. Some traditions have been defined such that modern ancestors are just applying the old thinking to new situations, but not able to add much innovation. Even so, evolution occurs. It is through this process of engagement and re-imagining that religions stay connected to the present and maintain some degree of relevance. The re-imagining of the ancestors of tradition is also a part of this process. The constant revisiting, and retelling of stories, the habit of interpreting the past anew in light of the present, is part of the means by which any tradition remains alive.

Once we settle on a single story, agree to it and carve it stone, there is no more life in the idea. Only truly dead ideas can be fixed ones. To be alive is to be in a state of flux and uncertainty. The more 'pinned down' a tradition is, the more inherent tension this creates, which can create swings from orthodoxy into rebellion and back. While we continue the process of debating our ancestors, dressing them up with new stories and re-making them in our own image, we are also engaged with the process of keeping them alive to us. I believe it was Oscar Wilde who said that the only thing worse than being talked about, is not being talked about.

We should not, therefore, be unduly troubled by this process of re-creation. As modern figures become historical ones, they too will no doubt be subject to the same retellings and ponderings, and so it will continue for as long as anyone is inter-ested in Druidry, or for that matter, any other tradition.

It's not only Scheherazade in the Arabian Nights who is kept alive by storytelling. It is every relationship and every community of storytelling creatures. This is the art of telling ourselves who we are. Just as love cannot be made once and then set aside as done in an amorous partnership, so story equally cannot be just told once and set down. In the telling and retelling, stories grow larger than their origins. They develop into myths and legends that give shape and identity to not just individuals, but communities as well. If Druidry is to thrive, then we will keep coming up with new stories about how it works, where it came from, and who our ancestors of tradition really were.

Chapter Nine

Working with the Ancestors

At the beginning of this book I referred to the brief way in which ancestors tend to be honored in current Druid ritual and said that I felt it insufficient. This chapter will explore various ways in which we can work more deeply with ideas of ancestry, how we can consciously construct our ancestors, how we can intentionally change our relationships with them to facilitate healing, and how we relate to the dead.

For the purposes of this chapter, I will mostly be using 'ancestors' to cover those of blood, place and tradition without particularly specifying any group within that, or considering any specific period of history. This does not mean that when we come to work with the ancestors, it will always be appropriate to relate to them as one homogenous lump. In all ancestral work, there will be much to gain from thinking of specific groups in their context, and sometimes considering individuals. There are times when the nodding bluebell head sea of the myriad grandmothers will be the image we need to contemplate, but where possible I would advocate a more specific and considered view of the ancestors as we approach them.

The first question to ask as we embark on this, like any good child, is, why? Why work with the ancestors? Who are we doing this for? Do we imagine that our words, rituals or actions benefit them? And, if so, in what way? There are many ways of understanding the nature of time and the afterlife, all of which will inform how we see the dead most especially. Are the ancestors still with us in some way, or influenced by what we do? There are no right answers here, but it makes the work considerably easier if you know how it fits into your own world view.

I can only comment on it personally. Much of my world view is underpinned by a keen sense of doubt and uncertainty. I have no idea if my ritual actions would be of any benefit to my ancestors, but equally I recognize I have no way of knowing that they aren't. I do know that my own stories and thoughts inform my behavior, and that my understanding of the ancestors is part of this. Therefore in terms of self-development and personal honor, my relationship with the ancestors is as important as any other relationship I may choose to consider and work with.

I am exploring my ancestors because I wish to learn from them, to avoid replicating their mistakes, to celebrate what was good about them, and to root my own life in a sense of the past. I do not imagine my ancestors will gift me with much direct wisdom or intercede with the gods (if there are any) on my behalf. They have existed, they continue to exert an influence, and they interest me. These are reasons enough for me, and after that I will simply see what comes of the endeavor. But having said all of this, I write this on a day of personal difficulty that comes after months of being challenged to breaking point. I have in my pocket the pentacle that belonged to someone who felt himself to be my craft parent (it's a long story) and my great grandmother's wedding ring, which my grandmother wore for many years. Tangible connections with ancestors of blood, place and tradition. When I am in pain, that gives a degree of comfort. No solutions, no hope, just the certainty that they were people who endured as much as they could, for as long as they could. None of them were quitters and all of them faced some dire setbacks in their lives. If I can be as strong as they were, I could ask no more than that.

There is nothing we endure that the ancestors have not already been through. The precise details can change, but the human experience, is, I believe, more constant than not. This is part of my story of the ancestors, that their emotions would make sense to me, and mine to them.

There are no right or wrong reasons for seeking the ancestors, so long as we honor them. The only wrong answer seems to me to be to try to ignore all of them and imagine that we live untouched by their influence. That seems insane. We exist in the impossible to capture moments between what was and what will be. 'Now' is one of the most difficult things to truly perceive. We look back, and we look forward. We cannot live in either of those other places, in the past or the future, yet both can be with us, all the time. That's a possibility with as much potential to enrich as to distress. Another one of those experiences that can turn you into a poet, or a lunatic. We are here and now. Everything else is behind us, and in front of us and time is very likely an illusion brought on by too much thinking. I think.

Choosing our stories

We choose which stories define us. These may be stories of race and place, or of blood heritage and tradition. In practice we are going to ignore or reject the vast majority of material available to us simply because there is too much of it to contemplate, much less work with. The process of deciding what to keep, what to explore and what to skim over needs to be a considered one. There are no specific right answers as we each quest after our own stories, but the person who works deliberately and mindfully will remain in control of their story. If we pay no heed to the stories that shape us, we have no power of them.

I find in all things it makes most sense to follow where the heart leads. If certain periods, figures or groupings are appealing, these are the best ones to explore. That can lead to romanticizing and to papering over the challenges, but working on things that make us miserable is hard to sustain, or for that matter, hard to justify.

There are many ways of working with the ancestors, from visiting the places they used, to re-creating their modes of working or costume. I feel closest to my grandmothers when I am making jam or marmalade, or cooking up a Christmas pudding, because I know they too did these things, and in much the same ways. I feel closest to my ancestors of place when the boat is moving, and we are travelling as narrowboat people have done before, for more than a century. My ancestors of music tradition are closest when I am playing or singing. Activity is a great source of both empathy and insight. We might not be re-enacting precisely, but none the less it creates a sense of connection and a basis for knowing that is not entirely academic.

> *There was much drinking, toasting, oath-taking, re-forging of bonds*
> *that would protect the clan through the hard times to come....*
> *Hangovers are the same now as they were then – one way we connect*
> *with our ancestors!*[47]

Out of these experiences, we can add our own insight to the stories we have about ancestral lives. Spending time hand washing, cooking from scratch and otherwise living in a way more akin to my grandmothers than contemporary existence, I think I know how much tougher life was for them. I know about the grind of work that's never finished, but I also know the relief of good drying weather, the pleasure of doing a small thing well. I know one great grandmother made an art form out of every domestic chore she had, with complex rituals around every job, and strict demands on how it should all be done. I doubt she would have approved of my sloppier ways of working.

This is not to say that we should go through our lives forever looking over our shoulders and trying for glimpses of history. Part of choosing the stories we tell, is choosing what percentage of our time and energy to give over to that vast expanse of time behind us. It is equally possible to define ourselves in terms of intentions and all that we imagine we will be. For children and teenagers, the sense of self has far more to do with the future than the past. As we grow, and time behind seems longer than likely time ahead, that focus can shift. In truth we need both, but the balance is individual, and needs to allow us plenty of space for the flow of that vital and elusive experience that is 'now'.

Pick your ancestral stories as though your life depends upon them. It does. At least in part.

Listening to the ancestors

Living ancestors are available for conversations, but often it's only after they have died we start to realize how much we never asked. Most ancestors have disappeared into the mists of history, their names and dates obscured, their voices apparently lost to us. Seeking the voices of ancestors is a strange business and vulnerable to our own subjectivity. We hear with our own ears, and will all too easily hear what we want to. As with all of the more imaginative Druidic work, listening to the ancestors calls for an open heart and as little personal agenda we can muster. The less we specifically want to get from it, the more chance we have of a valuable experience.

If we go to the ancestors in ritual or meditation, expecting either wisdom or an ego massage, we are wasting our time. There is no reason to assume that any given ancestor is better placed to understand and resolve our problems than we are. They have found, or not found, solutions to the issues in their own lives. They may have nothing of particular use to bring to bear. However, the ancestors are all people who have, to some degree, survived. They have lived, and know something about living. The wisdom they have to give us is far more about embracing the experience of life, I think, than any specific ways of dealing with it.

I suggested earlier that our lives are the consequences of all those ancestral couplings and that the astounding improbability of our being here is something to take to heart and rejoice in. That does not mean our ancestors will feel the same way about us. We may not represent the pinnacle of their hopes and aspirations. We may not be everything they strived for made manifest. It is entirely possible that we will disappoint. There is nothing to be gained by casting ourselves as eternal children and the ancestors as an infinity of parents who can be called upon to soothe and encourage us. If in the quest for ancestral voices, it becomes apparent this is what we want, it may be worth pausing and examining more immediate relationships to locate the source of this feeling and find more immediate and productive ways of facing it.

How then might we go about hearing the ancestors?

As I've explored the three kinds of ancestors identified by Druidry, I've talked about the ways we might know or encounter them. Any point of contact that feels resonant, is an opportunity for hearing. It might be a case of listening for ancestors in the land, in graveyards, or in objects that were precious to them. We might hear them in their sacred sites, or seek for their voices in the wind.

It may be that the process of trying to listen results in nothing, or equally in too much. We may find ourselves overwhelmed by a sense of presence as the ancestors seem to permeate all things, and the sense of spirit in every part of existence becomes clear. It is important to remember that the quest for spiritual insight is not a quest for ease. It is also important to remember that you do not get extra points for spiritual masochism, and that if something is unbearable, it may be better to choose not to bear it, or to come at it in more measured and functional ways.

I can speak to this from a degree of personal experience. I grew up partly in my grandmother's house, which had belonged to her mother before her. My great grandmother was such a distinct presence there that it never occurred to me things could be otherwise. The presence of ancestors seemed natural to me as a child, and normal in ways I now suspect it isn't. However, through my childhood to my early twenties, the idea of ancestry did not excite me that much. I'd ticked the 'witchy granny' box and was too busy living in my future. It was the experience of having a child of my own, that sent me back looking for my own blood lines. Becoming an ancestor in such an obvious way redefines where any of us stand with regards to our own ancestry, and in me it created a new consciousness of all the parents who had gone before. For others, different life changes and brushes with mortality might create the same impulse.

Being in the part of the world my blood ancestors came from has rekindled a sense of connection for me. I could not have made any serious connection with my blood ancestors while I was living on foreign soil. I was a mere sixty or so miles away, but the land had no relevance to me and no resonance. As I've commented before, I think there is a vital link between blood ancestry and how many of us relate to the land. Again this was a thing I didn't consciously know until I moved back into the landscape of my childhood. The issue of blood ancestry loomed large and became important, as did the idea of making my child more conscious of his own heritage within this space. He had a new landscape to learn. All those stories of place I had carried became his, and I watched him fall in love with this place that is so luscious with narrative and tales of his grandparents. Through story, this has become his place, and his blood ancestry has become more real and resonant to him. I've seen how, during a time of upheaval, these connections have given him stability and a sense of self.

Spending a winter in a cottage on the Severn's flood plain, I became aware of my ancestors as never before. Particularly at night when I couldn't sleep for anxiety, I often felt a keen sense of their presences. They were, for me, in the mud, and there were far more of them than I could distinguish. Sensing or imagining them gave me a kind of comfort. It resolved nothing and I did not think they could help me directly, but they were there, like the friend who sits with you while you are deep in grief, and makes no judgments. Sometimes, that is enough.

Even during times when I've been working with items belonging to my blood family, or in places made intense by long and deliberate use, I have never heard ancestral voices as clear speech. I do hear them though, most usually as an emotive murmur, a sense of connection and presence with maybe a hint of sympathy or encouragement. If there is one word, it is 'endure' and if there is a message for me, it is that this, too, can be borne. There are times when I want nothing more than to lie down and give up, but my sense of the ancestors certainly doesn't encourage that. I lie down for a bit, then I crawl up and attempt to keep going.

No doubt the experience of listening will be different for everyone who tries it, and will work differently also according to external events in your own life. If I needed less I might, paradoxically, be open to experiencing more. In the openness, in the silence of waiting to see if there is anything, we know ourselves to be the people who try to listen. We are the ones who reach out to the dead and who are willing to hear their voices without fear or judgment. This too becomes part of the story of self, and if the ancestors gift us with nothing else, they reliably give us the opportunity to be the kind of people willing to take heed of them.

Honoring the ancestors

There is considerable scope for honoring the ancestors in ritual, going far beyond the few lines we normally include in regards to them. Samhain would be an obvious focus, but every ritual brings us into direct contact with our ancestors of tradition. I think there would be much merit in including, in ritual, acknowledgement of the individuals whose words we borrow. It would be a gesture of respect, would provide those new to the path with valuable information, and would keep in our minds the human inspiration we are working with. Unattributed material can gain a bizarre authority or sense of antiquity it does not merit.

Every ritual we undertake brings us into contact with

ancestors of place – human and non-human. This consideration can be explored in detail, with creative and fact-orientated approaches. Taking time to reflect on who was here before and how we relate to them adds layers of meaning and connection into a ritual.

The focus on a wheel of the year narrative in the conventions of modern Druid celebration, makes it difficult to explore in depth stories not readily ascribed to some aspect of the process. At which point in the cycle would it be appropriate, for example, to honor our own blood ancestry – the living, not the dead? I think there is much to be said for stepping outside the sun cycle stories to undertake rituals that are then able to find their own form.

I once led a non-seasonal ritual focused on non-human ancestors of place – most specifically the creatures from our landscape that are now entirely extinct, or absent from their former haunts in the British Isles. We each brought our own material, each focusing on a specific creature. Content ranged from natural history, to song, poetry, art and storytelling as we each evoked and honored our chosen creature by our own means. It was a memorable ritual, rich in inspiration and created a basic model that can be revisited for all kinds of themes. We had intended to explore ideas of place in a similar format, working with local myths and place names to devote a ritual to stories of the land. I'd also envisaged working with tribe stories in just the same way, giving each participant opportunity to identify the ancestors of tradition they wanted to explore, and to express that relationship in any way they wished.

Ritual gives us tremendous opportunity to share our inspiration and creativity. There is no need to work with a single coherent world view or belief system within a ritual context. We can tell a multitude of overlapping, interlocking, even contradictory stories about our ancestors, offering what we know in the safety of circle. By sharing our stories, we keep them alive, by speaking them we place ourselves within them. Ritual gives participants a reason to explore ideas that might otherwise have not occurred to them and, in hearing each other's stories, we gain new perspectives on our own tales.

Working meditatively with ideas about the ancestors can also be a feature of ritual. I've explored the role of meditation in depth in Druidry and Meditation[48] so will only tackle the subject superficially here. Deep contemplation of any subject can contribute to your Druidic path. Working in meditation we can examine any of our stories about ancestry and its influences upon us. Any of the concepts raised in this book have the potential to be good sources of subjects for meditation, and no doubt there are many more besides.

We might work more imaginatively by contemplating facets of our ancestors' lives, creating visualizations of them as individual people, or the lines of our ancestry stretching back through time. If there is pain or difficulty around the issue of ancestry, then meditation can be a good tool with which to tackle this and attempt reconciliation.

If you have an altar, then you might consider including some ancestral representations as part of it, or even developing a space entirely devoted to the ancestors. It's interesting from a bardic perspective to contemplate what kind of image or other expression captures our understanding of ancestry. In trying to depict them, we are also depicting something of our feelings about them and how we wish to stand in relation to them. Making something can be a powerful way of embodying the ancestors and reconsidering relationship with them. Not only do depictions of them work in this regard, but also projects undertaken in the forms we know they used. That could be carving in wood or making a traditional quilt, and any number of other actions. The resonance of the undertaking matters more than both the logic of it, and the finished work. Bardic work can be a journey in its own right, not necessarily aiming for the destination of a finished piece.

Living ancestors

Last winter I went with a group of people to sing Christmas carols in care homes for the elderly. It struck me then that the vast majority of our elders in England are simply disappeared. When they are no longer able to fend for themselves, we bundle them off into homes and unless you have an aging relative to visit, the odds are you will never see the numbers of people from previous generations who are still with us.

Life expectancy has not been a constant across time or class. Wealth remains one of the best indicators of how long you might live. There seems to be increasing numbers of people surviving beyond a hundred, thanks to medical interventions. As a culture we seem entirely at ease with the idea that longer life is by definition good, but ask few questions about quality of life, or the conditions in which we expect our elderly to live. Like so many other vulnerable groups of people, our living ancestors, the ancient amongst us, are largely hidden from view. Whatever stories they have will go with them.

I watched a friend of mine struggling to keep her father at home after her mother died. Her father had Alzheimer's, and mercifully little idea what was happening, but part of his confusion included no idea where his wife was. The strain of supporting him and caring for the man's physical needs was more than my friend and her sister could hope to bear – not while needing to hold down full-time jobs. I watched my grandmother going through similar struggles trying to support an older cousin, and then her own brother with the trials of advancing age. There comes a time when professional help is needed, or more help than can be sourced within the immediate family. Admitting defeat is agony, and also relief, and the guilt surrounding that relief is also a terrible thing to be faced with.

One family facing this has limited choice. One lone Druid

wanting to engage meaningfully with living ancestors might be able to put in some voluntary work, but won't change the system either. It is not merely the system that needs challenging, but the whole idea we have as a culture around age, infirmity and value. In prioritizing financial activity, we priorities paid work, and therefore undervalue unpaid caring undertaken within families. We also undervalue those no longer able to earn a living. The end of a working career does not mark the end of contribution to society. Many retired people care for their grandchildren, save governments a fortune in other care bills, work as volunteers and give back in ways that no one in officialdom has bothered, so far, to properly consider. Just that a person exists should be enough reason to care for them, treat them with respect and support their dignity.

When someone is unable to work and needs caring for – and for most of us old age will bring this if nothing else does – we label them 'dependent'. What greater shame is there than to be unable to fend for yourself? To not be able to pay your way? To need someone's help with going to the toilet and all the other most personal, intimate activities? Why should there be this shame? There is none over the state in which we begin our lives – also in dependency. I am certain there are other ways of thinking about this that need exploring.

Collectively we fear getting old, so we don't talk about it too much and we certainly don't want to look at it. We herd the elderly off out of sight and most people will have no direct contact with extreme age and its attendant ailments until they have to support their own parents or face it themselves. Could we create a different way of valuing the old and aging? Might there even come a point at which we could say that it rightfully falls to the rest of us to take care of those who need it? Could we replace ideas of burdens with visions of compassion and duty? The measure of a human life is too often caught up in the prices paid or the tax collected. If we could step away from those money-led attitudes we might learn to value our elders for their own sake.

We don't recognize age. We don't respect it, value it, or even reliably treat it with compassion. Therefore as we contemplate distant ancestry we should also give thought to the ancestors amongst us. How do we, personally, treat the elders of our communities? How do we handle aging and its demands within our own family? Do we see it as fearful and burdensome, or are there other narratives to construct around the experience?

One of my Druid friends spoke to me at length about the challenge of finding she had to mother her own mother, and the impact of this changing role. The one who has been dominant, now becomes dependant. The one who has been mothered and sheltered must now step into the role of provider. Becoming something like a parent to your own parent is an experience I've not had, but potential for it exists for most of us. How will we adapt when called upon to take up that responsibility? Do we have the space and resources to do it?

I know of women who have given up home, relationship and work to go back to care for aging parents, or whose entire youth was spent in the parenting of parents rather than the raising of their own offspring. More often than not, the work seems to fall to daughters, and this is another aspect worthy of proper consideration. Unpaid caring work is undervalued, and usually defaults to women. It may be a chicken and egg scenario – is it undervalued because women primarily do it, or do women do it because it is not valued enough for men to be interested? Where care work is paid, it is not well paid despite being a physically demanding job with great responsibilities. If rates of pay equate to social value, then caring for the elderly is not work we think very much of at all.

Often it's far easier and more comfortable to think about ancestors in distant, abstract terms. The real and immediate ones will keep challenging us. These relationships too need our proper consideration, and not just in terms of the stories we tell to ourselves. We need to consider the entire narrative our societies have about aging, work and illness, and how these also shape our understanding of the issues. We need to ask if the collective vision we are building – life at any cost, little attention to quality of life, and no value for those who undertake the strenuous work of providing support to those in their final years – is a good one. What does this say about our values as a culture?

The ancestral dead

In Tewkesbury museum this summer I came face to face – as best I could, with the skeleton of a Roman woman. She was lying, as so many remains do, in a wood and glass exhibit case in a small, local museum near the site that had held her remains down the centuries. Seeing bones is always very emotive for me. It makes the life and death of history real and immediate. I experience a profound sense of connection with the dead when encountering them so directly, and at the same time I am troubled, repulsed, horrified and frequently confused by how we relate to the bones of the dead. This is an area in which I have yet to construct a clear narrative of my own. Hopefully this means I can pick through the arguments in a fairly even-handed way.

Modern dead versus ancient dead

We have entirely different attitudes to our own dead, in comparison with the long departed. Death is generally kept out of the public eye and recent human remains are afforded a great deal of respect. Digging up the recently dead is a source of horror and alarm. We go to great lengths to give the dead a decent burial or cremation, and to dispose of their remains in a way they would have approved of. The assumption is that the dead should be allowed to rest undisturbed, unless there is a good scientific reason to dig them up. The removing of body parts from the dead for research or transplant needs permission and families are expected to be horrified if it comes to light that their departed one was buried minus an internal organ, or even some tissue samples when permission for this was not expressly given.

When my mother wanted my grandmother interred in the same grave as her parents, she had a lot of difficulty achieving this, because closed graves should not be opened for fifty years, and a mere 48 had passed, give or take. The recently deceased, the dead whose names we know, we leave in peace.

I remember years ago there was a great deal of controversy over an exhibition, part art, part science, that involved a lot of human corpses. At the time I couldn't imagine why anyone would want to go and see it – the whole project sounded grotesque. The idea of walking into a museum or art gallery and looking at a recent corpse, stuffed and mounted perhaps, or pickled for posterity, is almost unthinkable. Society at large would be outraged, horrified, and morally indignant. Yet the ancient dead are commonplace exhibits.

There is this curious process by which the ancient dead become less real to us in some way. It can't be the simple issue that bones look less like people, because the bog bodies and Egyptian mummies still have a degree of flesh, and we aren't collectively outraged by them.

I gather that if a Christian burial site is excavated, the remains will eventually be reinterred with all due ceremony. The same is not true of pre-Christian bodies.

There are some very interesting differences between how we feel about the ancient, and the recent dead. They do not need to be our own ancestors to elicit this kind of response, either. Perhaps the recently dead bring us too close to our own mortality while the long departed are too far removed to unsettle us. Perhaps we value recent humans more than historical ones. The issue may be more to do with the living relatives, which the ancient dead are not always assumed to have, although this too can prove more complex. There is some sense that the impact on living relatives needs to be considered, and few of the ancient dead have living relatives who can self identify as such. This is no doubt a factor in how they are viewed by law.

In the UK, we can leave bits of ourselves to the organ donor program, but it's still not wholly within our control. A friend observed to me, 'I signed up to donate my brain and spinal column to MS research, which involved getting written consent from my next of kin. It's not enough that *I* will it. Because once I am dead, my next of kin can OVERRULE my wishes because it's the sensitive topic of brains, and it will have to be removed within 48 hours.' The next of kin have the right to determine what happens to a body after death, but once the body is disposed of, all rights evaporate. I have no idea what the legal arrangements are in other countries, I would assume similarity in English speaking places and Europe, but where attitudes to the dead are different, laws may also vary. I think about the mass graves of monstrous regimes, and the way in which this theft of the dead can itself be an act of oppression and brutality.

Learning from the ancient dead

Pagans, more than any other group of people I think, stand to benefit from what science and archaeology might tell us about the lives of our ancient pagan ancestors. Pagans are also the people most likely to resent the digging up and studying of ancestral bones in the UK.

There is currently a significant split in the community. Some pagans actively campaign for the reburial of bones, while others campaign in favor of archaeological research.

The argument for lifting and retaining bones is that while we can undoubtedly learn from them now, we may learn more in the future as new technology and scientific techniques come along to shed light on the past. We'll pause here for a nod towards the narrative of progress. Reburial, from this perspective, is tantamount to vandalism, throwing away vital resources that might yet give precious insight.

The other argument says that these remains hold something of the spirit of our ancestors. They belong to a specific landscape, and it is spiritually wrong to remove them from it in the first place. These are often bodies that were carefully buried by people we know had complex practices around burial. The existence of such complexity suggests that they cared about burial and probably wouldn't like being dug up and used in this way. We should put them back with the same respect afforded to Christian burials. It is disrespectful to our ancestors to keep them in museum exhibits, or worse yet, in boxes in basements.

The bones in boxes story may in fact be a myth. I've heard people speak passionately against it, and equally passionately, others in a position to know have denied it even happens much.

How do we weight the knowledge we might gain from ancestral bones, against the rights of those ancestors to remain in the soil? How do we determine what those ancestors would have wanted, or whether they would even care? Do we imagine them as being affected by the treatment of their bones, or has the spirit long since moved on? A part of how we come to this issue depends on what we think death means and where we think spirit resides. These are not questions we will ever have clear cut answers for, making the whole debate unavoidably subjective.

Animal dead

Natural history museums contain dead animals as exhibits. While these days animal bodies tend to be sourced in ethical ways, older collections will include creatures who were slaughtered precisely so that their skins could be stuffed and put on public display. For a long time, this was the only way an ordinary person could hope to see an exotic creature. There may be some arguments to make for the educational value of these collections, but they exist primarily to entertain.

Exploring the museum in Worcester, I saw an elephant's foot in one of their cabinets – a popular Victorian trophy brought back by travelers. These elephant feet were treated, had a cover put on the top and were used as umbrella stands. Stately homes often have hunting trophies on the wall, from large and more local deer to exotic big game again brought home as a memento of foreign travel. Tiger skin rugs adorn the floors of many a big house. For a long time, animal remains have been used as status symbols, showing off the hunting prowess of the owner and demonstrating the financial capacity to travel abroad in search of such exotica. To me it seems less about the beauty of the creature on display and far more about the ego of the owner. Trophies from this kind of private collection also find their way into modern museums, as with the elephant's foot example.

Stuffed animals are not just a throwback to Victorian collectors. Recently at a country fair I saw heads on plaques and birds in jars offered as house decoration. Generally speaking we find the use of human remains as decoration to be at best macabre, but the idea of keeping an animal corpse because it is pleasing to look at does not reliably engender the same reaction. My grandmother even had a brooch which had been made out of a hummingbird's head, and such decorations were not unusual in their time. Current sensibilities, and fashions would preclude wearing bits of animal as human decoration, but the days of the lucky rabbit's foot are not that far behind us.

We view dead animals as being wholly different from humans. No doubt this is in part because eating animals is normal and eating humans isn't. What humans do to animals is, in our collective understanding, entirely different from what we might expect to do to each other. We use animal skins for shoes and clothing, animal parts find their way into all kinds of other products too. Why shouldn't we stuff them and present them as attractive objects?

I've included this topic largely because I think it makes such a fascinating comparison. Our attitude to dead animals is so far removed from our attitude to dead humans, except where there is personal relationship. We bury and cremate beloved pets in just the way that we do people, sometimes even erecting little headstones for them in the garden. We wouldn't use the pelt of a dead family cat for clothing trim, nor, I think would the recent ancestors who collected animal trophies. There is a sense of 'us' and 'them' in the animal-human relationship that is not entirely clear cut. Animals are generally 'other' except where we designate one special creature as deserving human-like status. It implies an interesting flexibility in the way we can think about creatures. We can keep food animals as pets. Keeping them as pets, we can still eat very similar animals without any difficulty. It's also worth noting that European colonials had no trouble treating the ancestral human remains of colonized peoples as trophies and collector's items too. We might not frame and mount them in exactly the same way, but I don't think there's always much in it.

My own response to stuffed animals in museums is not unlike my emotional response to human remains. However, I'm not particularly affected by dinosaur bones. I find them interesting, but experience no real emotion on viewing them. Perhaps we have found the limits of my empathy here, perhaps the stone element of the bones affects my reactions, or perhaps it is the knowledge that humans did not kill them to make the exhibits that causes the different response. I'm not even sure why I respond as I do. I wonder to what extent this is true of other individual and collective reactions to the dead.

Ancestors in use

It is very probable that some ancestral bones were moved to barrows after the flesh had gone, and kept in a way that made them accessible to their tribe. There are plenty of stories about the Celts collecting human head, and skulls. We can only speculate why this might have been. There's an interesting, fairly modern comparison in the form of Italian monks who, short of burial space, dug up their own dead after a set period, used their bones to decorate the chapel and thus freed up the soil for the next corpse.[49] Clearly our ancient ancestors weren't short of space in the same way, which suggests a more spiritual reason for wanting access to the bones. Or am I guilty of assuming that because I can't make pragmatic sense of the activity, it must by default be religious?

This idea of keeping and working with human remains suggests that for our ancestors, it wasn't all straightforward either. Disposal of the dead so that we no longer have direct contact with them, is not universal. If we keep ancestral remains in public places, accessible to the modern tribe, might we in some way be in the same tradition as other communities who have kept their dead present? The bones connect us to the stories, and to the past. They make history real in a unique way. Should we be repulsed by the idea of dead people on public display, or should we welcome this opportunity to be more open about mortality, to meet death face on, and to connect in direct and immediate ways with the ancestors?

Appropriated dead

Not all of the dead who reside in museums can be said to belong to those who have taken them. Colonial history has involved the appropriation of ancestral bodies from all over the world, a practice that continued into the twentieth century. After a massacre in Namibia, German colonialists took hundreds of severed heads back to Germany for 'research' in what was probably the early stages of developing the pseudo-science of racial supremacy. These remains have only recently returned but are destined not for burial, but display as honored and heroic ancestors.

Under British law, people who can prove that they are the descendants of the bones can apply to have those remains returned to them. All of the arguments available for keeping the dead – about science, progress and learning could just as easily be applied to bones we have appropriated from other countries. That the UK government has created this law suggests an underlying belief that bones are still, to some degree, people not artifacts, and that as people they belong with their own tribe. Efforts to have the same law used on ancient pagan remains have run into difficulty not least because of the lack of readily identifiable decedents. British bones arguably belong to all of us, and we collectively don't know what that means.

Other cultures are far clearer about their ownership of stolen ancestors and the need to reclaim them. This is in part about much wider issues of colonialism and appropriation. There are so many things that cannot be readily undone or given back, that where it is possible, the action becomes iconic, I think. It is a way of symbolically tackling all those many things, the lives, ideas, languages, and cultures that were damaged, where the return is not so simple. I can only hope it brings a degree of peace to communities affected by the process. What I heard of radio broadcasting from Namibia suggested the return of bones brought hope and inspiration to people. The dead, the ancestors, are symbols of race and identity. If the oppressor owns the bodies of your people, the oppressor owns your history and identity as well. Taking it back gives more than the immediate remains.

However, Michelle Faul Windhoek, writing in October 2011[50] on this issue suggests that rather than bringing relief, it's fuelled yet more anger about historical German treatment of colonized people, and the near-extermination of the Herero people. Until I started exploring this topic I had no idea that these ancestral bones represented not only theft and abuse, but also genocide. When the wounds are so recent, the losses so horrendous and the history so emotive, the ownership of bones becomes ever more important, I think. While a return like this one may have opened up old pain, I also feel very strongly that it's hard to move forward without facing the past. How many other hidden genocides are there, waiting for the bones to reveal them?

In the case of the Torres Islanders' repatriation of ancestral bones, the BBC observed, 'They believe that until the bones are buried – the souls of their forefathers will not be able to rest.'[51] How do we weight this against another quote from the same article, 'critics say that the handover of the bones will set back scientific research and has been done for the sake of political correctness.' It takes me back to the quote I borrowed from Philip Carr-Gomm early in this book – that there are spiritual and material ways of viewing the past, and there is a choice to make between the two. There are times when we cannot have both, or honor both in full. But when so little remains of a slaughtered people, hanging onto remains for our science, in face of the emotional need of others, feels wrong to me.

Who owns the pagan dead?

The issue of who owns any dead people is a tricky one. In western society, everything is owned by someone. Dead people clearly no longer own themselves. Do their remains belong to blood relatives, the community, or the state? The ownership of next of kin is brief, and only lasts from death to disposal. The idea that organ donation in the UK should be compulsory would make all human remains here the property of the state, but at time of writing, that isn't the case. However, if you want to dig up a body, you have to apply to the Ministry of Justice for permission. All things considered, I think it's fair to say that if a branch of government has the power to give or withhold access to the dead, then effectively it has ownership. Again I have no idea whether other countries have different laws around disinterment. Ownership of the dead is not purely about the long departed, and does have considerable relevance for the living, because there is our relationship with the state to consider here too.

How we understand the dead informs how we perceive the living. Are bones bits of people? Are bones people too, or does it take more to define their humanity? Our laws protect and priorities human beings over things deemed to not count as human beings, so where we draw the lines has considerable implication. How do we decide that something isn't human, or no longer counts as human?

The dead have the potential to save lives in the direct form of organ donation. Research into the bodies of the dead has the potential to be very useful to medical science. Who knows what we might ultimately be able to extract and recycle? The information gleaned from dead people might have a market value – does that belong to family, state, or researcher? The ancient dead may also be providing us with information of contemporary relevance. Who owns the revenue from that? To the best of my knowledge, there's nothing clear cut out there.

Dead people can become tourist attractions. The graves of the famous get their share of visitors, and the contents of burial sites sustains interest in many a museum collection. Here too someone may well be making money out of the dead. Being dead, we suppose they won't care too much about this, but sometimes descendants do.

If dead people are within the land that you own, do you also own them? If they've rotted down nicely and left no discernible trace then of course you do, although you'll never know and no one will ever challenge it. If, however, something remains and is, for any reason, brought to the surface, are they still part of the owned land? In British law, certain finds (gold particularly) belong to the crown, so ownership of the land is not a clear indicator of possession. You can buy land whilst someone else retains the right to mine it, or to exploit certain resources should those turn up in it. As far as I know, purchasing contracts don't tend to involve sub-clauses about bones, but perhaps they should. It is interesting to consider what a personal response to inadvertently digging up an ancestor would be.

There are some modern pagans who want to be able to claim the ancient pagan dead as their own. Everything I have said before about the ownership of history, story and identity is just as true here. If the state, a museum, or a tourist attraction owns the bodies of the pagan dead, they own the history, and it is their understanding of the bones that will influence their fate. For example, Lindow Man has long been described by the British Museum as being a victim of Druidic sacrifice, as commented before. This official story is very different from the one Druids tell, but we do not have the bones, or the ownership.

Some modern pagans feel entitled to claim ancestral pagan bones for themselves, or see it as reclaiming the pagan-ness inherent in the bones, and liberating them from the grasp of a materialist, rationalist culture that cannot engage with them in any meaningful way. Others want the insight the bones might give, and there are plenty who have no strong feelings either way, based on what I've heard anecdotally.

If we had a clear line through history connecting ancient pagans to modern ones, we might have a legal claim on the bones of our ancestors. We don't. There is an argument that the ancient pagan dead belong to everyone, and that no single community, modern pagans included, should be given exclusive ownership. Is this a parallel to the issue of colonially appropriated bones, or an entirely different problem?

Bones in the British landscape at least have the potential to be ancestors of anyone and everyone. This is true across Europe. History has plenty of migrations and invasions in it making any idea of unadulterated continuity a bit shaky. Where there are strong ties of continued culture between the dead and the living, it's easy to place the bodies in a context and to give the living inheritors of tradition more say in what happens. Most of the time, it's just not that simple.

For all that modern pagans may want to believe we are the

inheritors of ancient pagan religion, we can't prove it to a degree that would give us the same rights as indigenous people who want their ancestral bones back. Not all modern pagans believe that we have any claim on the bones of our pagan ancestors anyway. Many are ambivalent about the subject. About the only consistency of opinion I've encountered is that whatever we do with the bones, we ought to treat them with respect.

There has been a tendency to take bones out of their landscape and off to big, national, or centralized collections, or places of study. The pagan case is tricky to make, but the geographical one isn't. If a body is found in Gloucestershire and taken miles away to London for display, that is appropriation. The more recent trend when it comes to the British dead, is to keep them close to home. The Tewkesbury woman I described at the start of this chapter was a few miles at most from where she had been buried. Her life, her story and her remains stayed in the place where they have relevance and resonance. That seems more respectful and appropriate, to me.

I don't know how close to the burial site bones need to be in order to preserve that sense of connection, but close is definitely the way to go, as I see it. Whoever owns the bones, keeping them in the landscape of origin makes emotional sense, and resists the centralizing of story, and power. Local bones, for local people! My own feeling would place bone ownership at a community level, where community is defined more by geographical proximity to burial site than by blood heritage. I realize in this context I am assuming descendants of place to be more important than descendants of blood or tradition. Part of this is pragmatic – there's less subjectivity in 'place'. Of course some bones held in museums won't have a tag on them identifying their origins, but on the whole I think it would be workable.

Alongside ownership, is the issue of reburial. The desire to own tends to go with a desire to either rebury, or not rebury the ancestors. This seems a tad polarized to me, and I wonder if there are more nuanced ways of expressing ownership, and thinking about the uses we make of bones. The process of writing this has led me towards a feeling that I'm not desperate for reburial, but I feel very strongly about keeping bones near to their original burial site, and keeping them in the community that now exists there – whatever form that takes. I realize that part of what unsettles me about the bones in museums experience, is the glass case. I understand entirely that these are required to protect and preserve, but feel, nonetheless that I would rather be able to have direct, tactile contact with the bones.

It is also interesting to ask who owns the grave goods in these ancient graves? At the time of interment, they were objects belonging to the dead person or objects those doing the burying felt moved to inter alongside them, for some other reason. Ownership at the point of burial would seem to lie with the corpse, but the dead cannot, legally speaking, own anything in our current culture. Museums do not only hold the bodies of other people's dead, they also own the grave goods associated with them. Treasures put in graves were clearly there for a reason, and while artifacts, like bodies, have much to tell us about the past, I think we should consider this ownership issue too.

If the objects belonging to a person go into the grave because they are too much part of that person to be kept by others, then these items are also part of the person. If we think about presence in the land, objects are no less part of the land and the landscape than human remains. They are, arguably, part of the dead and it is only our modern habit of perceiving separation that allows us to think of these objects as being separate from those people they were buried with. As a culture we like separating things out into neat designations and giving them all labels. Some of our ancestors disposed of the dead in separate pieces, some buried things with them. The habit of thinking of things as separate is not universal. Letting the habits of our contemporary culture define how we treat the past is easy, but we stand to learn more if we can recognize our own defaults and the possibility that these are not shared with our ancestors.

Healing, changing, recognizing and releasing

If we try to make any claims for the needs of our ancestors, we are on uncertain ground. However, when it comes to dealing with our own issues, it's easier to have clarity. Post-colonial people need their ancestors back as part of a symbolic and literal reclaiming of their heritage and power. It's not necessarily about what the dead need, as they might not need anything at all, but undoubtedly allows the living to reimagine themselves and move on.

When we work with the dead, we are also working with ourselves. This can take a multitude of forms and will come from within, from need rather than external specification. No two stories will be the same here, so I'll talk in terms of broad themes and try to avoid anything too restrictive.

The first step to any work is having some idea of what it is supposed to achieve. At the outset, it isn't always possible to know where the work will go. However, intention shapes the choices we make, so knowing your own intention is very important. At this stage, simple thought forms may serve you best. 'I wish to heal myself.' 'I wish to understand.' 'I wish to make peace.' There might be several intentions tangled together, or we might find that one intention leads us into a whole new area of working. In any kind of work, positive statements are better than negative ones. 'I want to move on' is of more inherent use than 'I don't want to be like this anymore'.

Often it serves to keep those intentions broad – focused, but not too focused. If, for example, I start out my ancestral work with the intention 'I want to make peace with the history of drug abuse in my family' that might only get me so far, and might prevent me from seeing a wider context that I need to understand. In this imaginary scenario, I might not yet know that the drug abuse legacy has to do with child abuse, or mental health issues, or some other story hidden by the more apparent one. When we work with the ancestors, sometimes it's necessary to dig deep, looking for the bones of stories that make sense of experience.

In any kind of spiritual work, I would always advocate doing the practical, pragmatic things first. If there are people you can talk to about the past, go to them first. If there are documents to read, or places to visit, start there.

Once the pragmatic options have been explored, the real work happens inside. However we understand that, it is about internal changes. We cannot change the past, but if it can be understood in a different context, or put into a new perspective, that in and of itself may be liberating.

The ideas I raised in the title of this section are critical in ancestral work where there is any residual pain. The first stage is recognizing. In identifying what aspects of our ancestry we have issues with, we can look at changing not those relationships, but our understanding of them. I have an abusive relationship (not ancestral, but it makes a useful illustration) in my history. For a long time I understood that relationship to be one I held responsibility for. It was my fault things were wrong and I was merely being punished for failings. Through counseling and peer support I became able to change my perceptions, identifying that relationship as an abusive one. Guilt and shame are such normal responses to troubled backgrounds, and so many people carry that within them. Understanding the past can enable any of us to re-examine it and change our beliefs about it.

When we are able to think differently about something, it becomes possible to change how we feel about it. Intellectual changes are relatively easy to make, but getting that awareness in deeply is slower work. Feeling a thing is not so automatic, but will follow in time. It is in re-feeling our story that the healing takes place. The emotional understanding of what has happened shifts how we feel about ourselves, and from there we can move into the stage of releasing. Having owned and acknowledged the past, it becomes possible to let it go, and move forward consciously, without it hampering us so much.

This is not a process that calls for forgiveness. There is no requirement to accept or condone. It just means recognizing what has happened, understanding its impact, and becoming able to move away from it. Forgiveness is a choice, not an obligation. We can choose to accept, or to carry the anger with us. Knowing what it is and where it came from makes a world of difference.

I do not know if such work makes any difference to the dead. I do not know if there is an afterlife, or how near the spirits of the dead may be to us. Some people believe that ghosts exist because spirits have uncompleted business. Others believe that issues we have not resolved return to us in future lives, for us to face again. Whatever the shape of your spiritual path, it makes sense to actively resolve any conflicts you have and to address old pain. Life is hard enough without going through it dragging along all the baggage our ancestors have bequeathed to us. It may be that in making peace with the past, we are sparing ourselves trials in future lives, or allowing the dead to move on. We cannot know. My feeling is always that work of any kind should be undertaken for the worth inherent in it, not for any hopes of subsequent reward, and especially not reward in the 'hereafter'. No matter how distant the ancestors we may be working with, we are here and now, and the experiences played out through this lifetime are the ones we must focus on. I am also wary of imagining any structure that gives us second chances. They may be a way of ignoring responsibility now, and pretending we can fix things another time, when the truth may be that no such opportunities exist. It is better by far, to get things right sooner, rather than later.

Not all ancestral work is about this kind of healing process, but it is the best place to start. I mentioned in the introduction an attempt at running an ancestral workshop. Pagans with too much pain in their recent ancestry were unable to think about their distant ancestors. Immediate history can be a very real block on emotional and creative access to the more distant past. It makes sense to resolve any more immediate issues before trying to move on. It may be that the idea of Christian ancestors, or other aspects of our deeper ancestry also need working through, which can be approached in much the same way.

From a position of feeling no immediate need or conflict, it is easier to work with the ancestors. We can be more open to their voices and ideas, because there is no desire to hear anything in particular. For some this might lead towards deep meditation, or work of a more shamanic and visionary nature. It is also possible to get to this point and, feeling no requirement in ancestral relationship, to let the whole issue of ancestry melt away, as attention moves towards some other area of need. There are no right answers, no ultimate goals of understanding or achievement to work towards here. It may make sense to hold ancestors in quiet relationship, with recollection and storytelling, but no deep work at all. The right answers are the ones that make sense at the time.

Chapter Ten

Ancestors of the Future

The future is not carved in stone so far as I know. I do not believe in a mechanistic universe in which all things are inevitable and in which the choices we make are the only ones that were ever available to us. However, the future is inevitably shaped by the present. The choices we make now inform the options we will have tomorrow. Not only does this have implications within our own lifetimes, it has huge consequences for those who come after us.

We are the ancestors of the future. Even those who do not have children will still have descendants of place. Some of us will have descendants of tradition as well. It's easy to think of 'tradition' in terms of the living giants amongst us, figures like Emma Restall Orr and Phillip Carr Gomm or the recently departed Isaac Bonewits, whose names will no doubt be remembered and whose influence will continue for some time to come. However, everyone exists in relationship and through our connections we share our ideas. What most of us leave behind in terms of descendants of tradition will more likely be people who do not specifically remember us, but who absorbed something we said or were inspired by a thing we did. A legacy like that is something to aspire to, I think. To be a voice contributing to the continuation of a great song would be an honor indeed. There is more scope in being an ancestor of tradition than the small number of memorable names may suggest.

Every action we undertake has consequences. Every choice we make not to do something has consequences as well. Our lives all leave marks on the earth, and we all influence those around us. Even blood ancestry soon forgets its origins. In four or five generations names are lost and stories fade or evolve into myths. Not only can we not know what legacy we will leave, but we also won't know whether anyone will notice. That may sound like an argument for not bothering. Why think about being an ancestor of the future if no one is going to notice you?

Most of our historical ancestors have become invisible to us, yet we exist, and our world exists precisely as it is now because of them. Every choice made, every action undertaken, every move avoided. The world as we know it is the consequence of everything that has thus far happened within it. By this measure, nothing can be deemed irrelevant and so long as there is a future, we too will be ancestors.

It can be tempting to see yourself as the end point of the ancestral story, but none of us are. Even if we have no children, ancestry continues and our influence with it. None of us is the punch line. There are stories to consider here also. Whether we position ourselves as ancestors of the future, or not, has a lot of potential to shape what we do. Below are a selection of stories that place us in the ancestral lineage in different ways.

Future story number one

I am the end of the line. I'm the last one in my family, and also I am at the end of history. I'm the one living here and now, and what matters therefore, is me. The past is irrelevant and the future is not my problem. I owe the future nothing, and anything that is here, is available for my use. I am entitled to please myself, to take what I want, do as I see fit. If anyone does come after me, they will see themselves in the same way and do as they please as well. I am not responsible for them.

Future story number two

I will be the ancestor of nothing much. My kids don't listen to me now so there's no reason to think they will carry forward any ideas of mine. The world is a very big place, I am just one small, irrelevant person and in a hundred years' time no one will remember I existed, much less care what I did. So you see it doesn't matter very much what I think, or how I live, and whether I recycle my paper or not. There's only one of me and even if I change, I won't change anything, so why bother? Why not just enjoy my life? It's the responsibility of governments and big businesses to sort things out. Little people like me have no power; it's not fair to make us responsible.

Future story number three

I am the mother of invention, the father of revolution. I am one of the few people alive today who can say with certainty that they've changed the course of humanity. I have discovered a thing, or invented it, I have fixed a thing, or taken people in a new political direction. I am a hero, an icon, and because I know what I do matters, I pay attention to it. People listen to every-thing I say, and I'm going to leave a huge and very important legacy. In a hundred years' time, they will be teaching my life, my ideas as part of the school syllabus.

Future story number four

I am the keeper of the inheritance of future generations. I subscribe to the belief that we do not own the world, but borrow it from those yet to come, and so I see myself not as an end point, but as a beginning. What am I handing on? I want to be proud of what I've left behind, and to depart this world with a clear conscience. I will leave it better than I found it, having taken no more than I needed and having put in more than I took out.

If experience to date is indicative, the majority of people would place themselves in the first two stories, as the end of the line, or as ancestors of nothing much. These stories confer the advantage of never having to consider the longer term consequences of your actions. The less powerful we believe ourselves to be, the less responsibility we have, and the more freedom we then imagine ourselves to be granted, to live as we please. After all, what point is there in life but to enjoy ourselves? What could possibly matter more than our own wellbeing and happiness? It's not like we're going to be here to see what life is like for our great, great grandchildren, so why stress over it? Let them fix their own problems.

This is a philosophy of ease that justifies whatever abuses we care to heap upon the planet whilst allowing us to feel entirely self-righteous about it. One is born of supreme arrogance – the 'end of the line' notion, while the other, I think, has more to do with fear of what would happen if we recognized our own power. If we imagine that we can make a difference, to ourselves, much less anything else, what might we then be obliged to do?

There are people alive today who must know that they are indeed the mothers and fathers of inventions. They work in all fields, and see their influence catch on while they are still alive. Looking at the world leaders, the Nobel Prize winners, the great thinkers and innovators alive today, it's easy to see them as a race apart. These are indeed the future ancestors of tradition people will be taking inspiration from for generations to come. These are legends who stride through life while we mere humans just plod along. Seeing them in their greatness we might fool ourselves into thinking that these people were always something apart and their special status is just the natural consequence of this. They are the gods amongst us.

I could devote a whole book to exploring the idea of greatness, and where it comes from. For the purposes of contemplating being a future ancestor, I think the most important point is this. Most of the people who are 'great' probably did start out believing they were bound for wondrous things. Casting my mind back to childhood and my teenage years, I remember we all thought that. I don't remember any friends who aspired to be middle managers, office scutters, quality control officers, or impoverished single parents. We all knew that we were destined for greatness. Somewhere along the way, most of my peers evidently decided that wasn't going to happen after all. Life knocked them back, and they set their sights a little lower, a little more realistically, and carried on. Only a handful of the people I knew at school are doing the things they wanted to do, and being successful at it.

Conventional wisdom has it that it's not a good idea to pump young people's heads full of silly ideas. They can't all be the next pop sensation, the next big thing. Most of them won't make any difference at all. Going through the school system I learned very quickly that it was not wise to say I wanted to be an author. No kind of career path there, and clearly I wasn't going to manage to do that. The sneering 'is that even slightly realistic?' question knocks the aspirations out of so many young folk before they even get a chance to try. That's not realism, that's throwing opportunities away. I learned to say that I wanted to be a teacher, because that's a sensible looking profession. I'm still finding people suggest that I ought to stop being silly and get a proper job. I'm sure people have offered that piece of advice to every successful author, actor and musician who ever lived, to every aspiring politician, creative entrepreneur, and to anyone who dared imagine doing something no one had done before.

If we were all resolutely sensible, there would be no music industry or film industry, and no novels written. There would be no entrepreneurs, or explorers, and the leading edge of human knowledge would be a very quiet, seldom visited sort of place that would rarely change. The people who achieve great things are the ones who did not give up on themselves. The one thing that sets the gods amongst us apart from everyone else, is the unwillingness to give up on dreams and knuckle down to being sensible. The world would not just be a poorer place without these ancestors of future, it would be stagnant and devoid of color.

A person who takes themselves seriously and values what they do can enter any field of work, and transform what is supposed to be 'ordinary' into poetry and innovation. Creativity can be brought to bear in any activity, as can honor and a sense of excellence. The person who treats any aspect of their lives as art and as important creates far more than the mere job description would allow. This is a path that does not announce itself, and that sits alongside the mindset of the future custodian. To do something, anything, well because that is the right way to do it, not for the glamour and fame, or for the money, has a kind of heroism that is woefully underappreciated. It is a path available to all of us in our every waking moment. It depends on valuing ourselves and whatever we put our hands to.

How different would the world be if we each treated our normal, daily activities as things of singular importance? How much would our own life experiences be changed by this? What would it do to any individual's sense of self-worth? All we have to do is imagine that we matter, and that everything we do is significant. From this we can then go forward to perceive that everyone else matters too, and that everything everyone else is doing is also important. Not just what is done, but how it is done, and whether it is done well. This in turn enables us to notice excellence in small things, to celebrate it and affirm the efforts of those walking the path of living their art in the details of their lives. The act of celebrating inspired living on any scale then becomes an affirmation of that way of being, and an encouragement to continue in it. Every person who travelled this path would draw others along it with them, and nothing in this world would ever be the same again.

Not everyone is going to be the next Bill Gates. However, if we took ourselves seriously, imagining that how we live our lives matters, and placing ourselves in a story that means we are ancestors of future, we give ourselves more scope for achievement. Even if we take the less bombastic fourth story and fashion ourselves as custodians, we are still embracing the idea that what we do, counts.

What we do, matters.

All of it.

The myth of our own insignificance may be the most dangerous story we tell ourselves and it is certainly the one most to blame for the things we do not do.

For the purposes of this chapter I am writing with the assumptions that we should care about our status as future ancestors, and that as a society, we do not. Our politics are painfully short term, our collective behavior is unsustainable and at this rate if future generations survive to look back at us, they are unlikely to do so with any kind of gratitude or appreciation.

I would like to be remembered fondly, and to be an honored ancestor. I suspect I am not alone in this. Who would choose to be remembered as an example of how not to do things? My only hope in this regard is to live, as best I am able, in a way that has the potential to merit such recognition. It is not enough that I make sufficient noise to be remembered after I am gone. I would rather be remembered for living well, or not remembered personally, but have the work I have done survive me, and the things I have contributed to the world remain and be valued when I am not here. These do not need to be epic things either – the trees I have planted, and will plant, the charities I have supported, the tiny knock on effects of how I live from one day to the next – they all count towards what I hope to leave behind.

To be responsible ancestors of the future, the most important thing we can do, is care. All else follows from this.

Future blood ancestor

One of the biggest personal choices we may make, is whether to be a parent, a future ancestor of blood. Not everyone gets to choose consciously, but these days most of us manage to control our fertility. Choosing not to have a child is, biologically speaking, easy enough – in the sense that you can have surgery to ensure that you never do, if you feel that strongly about it. Sometimes wanting to reproduce does not result in parenthood, despite all of the available medical interventions. The choices are seldom entirely in our own hands, but the intent will likely shape how we experience what happens. For some of course there is no conscious decision. I felt from an early age that the decision to have sex was the decision to accept a possibility of parenthood, but this doesn't appear to occur to everyone, and again, some people get no choice.

In terms of available narratives to draw on, being a parent by choice is the benchmark for 'normal'. People are expected to want and have children – women especially so. Having a child has been the whole focus, the point of life for women and we have been defined in terms of it for a long time.

There are many reasons not to want a child. Many people simply don't feel they would make adequate parents, or cannot find a partner they consider suitable for breeding with. Gay and lesbian people sometimes want children, and sometimes don't, and for the 'don't' group, that can be very much about their sexual identity. People with inheritable diseases may decide they would rather not pass them on. Accident, illness and disability can all conspire to prevent parenthood, and for some falling pregnant does not lead to live birth, or to children who survive. This is nothing new. All of our family trees will have the aunts and the uncles in it, the ones who would not, or could not, have children of their own. Even so, it is still perceived as an odd choice and assumed to be a source of unhappiness. Can you live a full and happy life without having a child? Of course you can.

Being a direct blood ancestor should not be our only function in life, and I see no reason to priorities this to the exclusion of all other aspects of what it means to be human.

Whether we have direct blood descendants or not, we are still part of a family tree, and the odds are we have kin out there, even if we do not know them. Our current laws and social structures assume heterosexual, married, reproductive life as the default, but if the numbers of single parent families rise, the number of openly gay people increases and the number of people choosing not to breed, or unable to, increases, we may have to rethink our benchmarks for 'normal'. I am very much in favor of not designating non-breeding status as 'abnormal'.

For someone who wants but is unable to have children, this is an especially painful issue. I'd always imagined having two, so finding I would only have one biological child came as a blow. I found a surprising number of people felt entitled to question me about only having one, and a few who felt that in only having one child, I wasn't a really experienced parent. A normal family has two children, after all. So I can imagine what a childless woman might have to endure on that score. The grief of people who cannot reproduce can be vast, and the social pressure added to it is no help at all. The pressure on those who choose to be childless, who are called selfish and misguided to their faces, is obscene.

If you have blood descendants, then how you style yourself as an ancestor to them is of course very much open to individual beliefs, style and preference. Many people have wonderful parenting experiences. For a lot of folks, it's a struggle, littered with self doubt and anxiety. Some people give away their children, some abuse them or even kill them. A significant number of parents have such poor relationships with their children that once those offspring reach adulthood, they make themselves scarce, and never look back. I know of so many adults who are not closely involved with their own parents, or who went to considerable lengths and distances to escape from their influence, in several cases even citing parental relationships as a motivation for changing country!

Having blood descendants is no guarantee of having any kind

of relationship with your own bloodline into the future. Having supplied a new generation with genetic material is not, and should not, be a reason to keep a hold on them. Children are people too, and ones who can grow up to resent us, or fear us if we handle their growing badly. They also come without instructions and as birth rates fall, many people find their first experience of children comes with having their own. Only the memory of their own childhood is there to guide them, making it easy to pass on old mistakes to new generations.

Over the years I have shared stories with a great many people. Tales of parents and children have played a significant part of that. I've also been caught in the personal drama of several sons who want no contact with their fathers. Parents who, from the outside, can look entirely good and appropriate, can turn out to be none of those things from the perspective of the young humans they tried to raise.

I think one of the biggest mistakes we make as parents lies in assuming our children will be like us. They came from us, they may physically resemble us, and of course we want the affirmation of another living being reflecting back our perceptions of self. From the moment they arrive, children are complete and unique human beings, and they are not us. They think and feel in their own ways, and in trying to impose anything of us onto them, we run the risk of getting them very badly wrong. Accepting they are not us, and letting them be their own people from the first breath to the last is one of the hardest and the most important things we can do for our offspring. We can accept them, and give them space to be their own people.

The more you try to control the ideas, feelings and actions of a child, the more they resent you. It's so easy to do this unconsciously, especially when we wrongly assume that they are just like us. What would suit us, and make sense for us won't automatically fit them like some psychic second skin. Our best interests and theirs can turn out to be wildly incompatible. The things they dream of for themselves may very well turn out to make no sense to us. This does not give us the right to tell them not to.

There are so many stories those of us who breed may tell ourselves about the children we have, or imagine we will have. They are to be our immortality, our justification, our vindication. They will get right everything we get wrong, and do amazing things, but at the same time we may conversely be afraid of them passing us or moving out of our sphere of influence. So many people look at the very little ones and say 'I wish that they could stay that way forever' but the nature of children is to grow and change. The only children who do not grow up, are the ones who die before they get the chance.

The more stories we attach to a child, or a grandchild, the less room they have for their own. We shape them with our hopes and aspirations, perhaps we push them towards all the things we wanted and were denied. And here the path to hell can so readily be created out of our good intentions. We want the best for them, and if we start off with the assumption we know what that means, we will never hear their opinion on the subject.

When it comes to the stories we make about our descendants of blood, I think the most helpful thing we can offer them, is no story at all. Let them be who they are, and invent themselves freely. Our job is to accept and support them, not to fit them into the narrative we most fancy. It is in trying to pin our own offspring into our story, that we are most likely to drive them away, and that does not serve us at all, much less the future.

Future ancestor of place

This is the one form of ancestry we can be certain of. We are all the future ancestors of everyone else who is ever going to live on the earth, human and not-human alike. In this regard we are bound to impact on those who come after us. Even if it's on a small scale – like the way we affect the people who buy our house from us, or inherit it, we can be certain of leaving a legacy that continues beyond our lives.

We can think about this aspect of future ancestry in a number of ways. Firstly there's our impact on our immediate environment – home, garden, locality. What happens as a consequence of our being here? What do we plant, or cut down, sustain or damage? What thrives because of us, or dies because of us? This is our legacy as a future ancestor.

It's then possible to think more widely in terms of how our lifestyle choices impact on the wider environment – how much pollution do we cause, how many food miles or air miles do we tot up? What dies for us in distant places we will never see? What is the environmental cost of the clothes we wear, the hobbies we enjoy, the journeys we make to rituals?

This line of thought if carried through properly can be so depressing as to make it all seem pointless. I've heard plenty of pagans express the idea that sometimes it seems the most ethical thing we can do, is kill ourselves. I believe that all living things have a right to exist, and that includes us, and I do not think despondency is the answer. Sliding into misery over the effects we have, accepting our own powerlessness, we can go on to believe there is no point in trying, and therefore no need to try. It's a cop-out response, an abdication.

If we accept that every negative impact we have is part of our place as ancestors of the future, we must also accept that every good thing we leave behind us is part of that contribution too. Every item recycled, every tree planted, every act of composting, re-use, and mindfulness. None of us are going to be perfect, and living is unavoidably intertwined with consuming. We can, however, aspire to live lightly, to take no more than we need and to offset the harm we inevitably cause by whatever means we can.

If we look back at our ancestors of place it's apparent enough that they were driven to a fair extent by physical need, and by material greed. Although physical need also wreaks havoc with other life forms, it is more tolerable than action based on greed. It's hard to think of others when you are in extremis yourself. However, our standard of living is far beyond that enjoyed by our ancestors. We have the luxury of comfort, and we can afford to ask questions about our real needs, and to contemplate our place in the scheme of things.

We live in a culture so obsessed with money and possession that it pushes people into imagining needs they do not have. If you are giving up things you need in order to be a better ancestor of the future, that can be painful to the point of also being unsustainable. If you instead explore what need means, and re-evaluate your own life, then letting go of worthless acts of consumption becomes easy. This is not a hair-shirt philosophy, there is no requirement to suffer in order to be a better ancestor of the future. This is a vast subject, and I would recommend Enough is Plenty[52] as a book that explores the beauty of sufficiency in a most compelling way.

Our role as future ancestors of place is the one we have the most control over. It is the aspect of our personally legacy we each have most scope to define. Granted, anything we build can be knocked down, anything we make may be ruined, but that's no reason to not bother.

The life of self-serving indolence, where short-term personal comfort takes priority over all else, is the easiest to maintain from one day to the next. It takes no effort to throw out useable items, to waste food, be careless with energy use, drive everywhere, and so forth. Living carelessly and with no regard for future impact is the most straightforward choice and our societies go out of their way to facilitate it, and to sell us more goods that help us stay in the duvet running up the electricity bills. This is only possible because we live in luxury. People in true poverty in the world are still obliged to focus on the essentials of life. We forget, in our privilege, just how indulged and secure our lives are.

Caring requires effort and a willingness to put aside short-term personal indulgence. Selfishness is easy, but living with mindfulness of other life forms, of the future, of anything whose needs are different from ours, takes effort. We are continually encouraged not to do this: Buy now, pay later, because you deserve it, because you're worth it, because you should never know a moment of minor discomfort let alone any real challenge. Sacrifice is for fanatics. Selfish living is supported by the story that we can't change anything anyway. It is part of our deliberate abdication of personal power.

The person who gets out of the duvet, turns off the television, turns down the stupefying heat, and goes off to do something real, is a much happier person. There is no substitute for reality – real food, real relationships, real creativity. The person who plays at being a leader, a soldier, a spy or any other exciting entity in a computer game, has nothing to show at the end of playtime. They will be ancestors of global warming, and very little else. The world is full of challenges and adventures for anyone who dares to get out there and live them. The world is also full of beauty and wonder for anyone who turns off the computer and television for long enough to step outside and take a look. The legacies we make with our hands, and in our own lives are not just going to benefit those who come into the world after we are gone. They benefit us, now, because these are the ways of living that truly enrich us.

To be a responsible future ancestor of place, ironically what we need to do is start taking far better care of ourselves.

Future ancestor of tradition

Many of us set out with what is effectively the intention to be an ancestor of tradition. We become teachers, in our chosen field, passing down our own peculiar ways of doing and seeing things, in the hopes that others will take those ideas forward. Where the desire is for immortality of self rather than ideas, there can be significant conflict.

One of the things I discovered as a student was that I had no desire to be a carbon copy of any teacher. The more determined a teacher – in any field – was to make me into them, the more likely I was to go somewhere else. At college my favorite teachers were entirely happy to let me run off in my own directions. My first Druid teacher wanted a mini-me, and thought I looked like a suitable candidate. I was to absorb the knowledge given to me, without question, and do the things I had been told to do without asking why they were necessary. I came under pressure to dress in prescribed ways, to change my diet, and modify my beliefs. I did not stay there long.

As a teacher I have learned that the most interesting and rewarding students argue with me. They come back with questions, alternative interpretations, places my ideas wouldn't work. They pick holes in my arguments, or demand that I explain myself to greater degrees. Good students are hard work for the teacher, endlessly demanding, never passive receptacles, always pushing you to give them more. It can become a cycle of mutual challenge that is as valuable a learning experience for the one in the 'teacher' role as it is for the one ostensibly there to learn.

Good students do not swallow wisdom whole and trot off into the world like little disciples determined to spread the news of your brilliance. Instead, good students will take some of it on board, ditch a few things, turn a few ideas inside out and then come up with half a dozen innovations of their own. By the time they get out there talking to other people, you'll be lucky if you recognize anything of your own influence in where they've got to. This is how it should be.

Traditions are not fixed and permanent things. That it is possible to come into any tradition as a new voice proves this point. Why should we assume that our words mark the end of history? Of course it can be tempting to hope that yours will be the definitive work, the final say, the epic piece after which nothing more can be added. It won't be, and in many ways this is as well. Creating the final, definitive piece would end the tradition we belong to. When no one has anything new to add, what you get are museum pieces, and the flow of life goes somewhere else. Just as stories must be retold to keep them alive, so traditions must be reinvented.

I grew up exposed to the English folk music tradition. As a music genre, it has a lot of contemporary singer songwriters working in it. I think the greatest achievement a folk musician can hope for is to have their work enter the tradition. Every song and tune we have was written by someone, but time and sharing has parted the music from its creators. They become 'traditional'. While a modern singer songwriter is named and known, they have not become part of the tradition, it's only when the music takes off, gains a life of its own with no reference to them, that they are truly part of the tradition. Much the same could be said of the lives of fairy stories, jokes, and a whole host of other ideas. From a certain perspective, the creator's disappearance is a measure of their success. The ideas become so universal that the originator is lost from sight.

If we are part of any tradition, we can either seek to harness it for our own fame and gain, or seek to support it with little or no regard for personal profit. If it is love of the tradition itself which motivates us, then disappearing into it is akin to the idea of the soul blending into Nirvana. Becoming part of the whole and lost within it, but still contributing to it, is a beautiful idea. If, however, we are motivated by ego and a desire for personal fame, it's easy to undermine or betray the very thing we claim to be working for.

In thinking about this issue I'm put in mind of Iolo Morganwg, working with ancient texts and a vision of Druidry, fabricating texts to support his own theories and dishonoring his own tradition through his fraudulent work. Ronald Hutton describes him as seeking adulation and wealth for himself, wanting to advance his political and religious ideas for a better world, to make his part of Wales more famous and to increase the importance of Wales within the UK.[53] These then were likely his motivations in so deliberately seeking to be an ancestor of tradition. While he failed singularly to achieve wealth or adulation in his own time, he has turned out to be a significant ancestor of traditional for Welsh cultural Druidry, and spiritual Druidry. He's a prime example of how we can never know what time will do with our legacy, and the same may be said of Aubrey, grandfather of archaeology, whose writings were only important because of what others have done with them since he lived. Real service to a tradition seldom shows itself in a single lifetime.

All of us have the potential to be ancestors of tradition, even if that's not in such dramatic ways. By passing down a tradition, we enter into its ancestry and become part of it, along with all the other now-invisible souls upon whose labors the tradition itself has always depended. New movements start every day, but only those with a long lasting supply of these quiet ancestors, actually survive the death of their founder. It takes strong ideas, not personal charisma, to maintain a new tradition or a strand within an existing one. To carry on a tradition without seeking self-aggrandizement through it is a truly honorable undertaking. Often it is through the small innovations and quiet contributions of these not-famous ancestors, that the tradition itself truly thrives and grows.

Every aspect of life has its traditions, and we interact with them on a daily basis. Here our scope to contribute as future ancestors of any tradition, is vast. It is through the inspiration we share with others, the memes we redistribute, and the small modifications we make that we all contribute to the great flow of evolving culture. This is the life energy of all tradition and the most essential work. Any tradition can survive perfectly well so long as people are sharing it and keeping it alive. No tradition requires famous people to hold it together. I cite as an example here the St John's Ambulance Brigade, with a long history of medical charity and training. I can't think of a single 'big name' associated with it, but it continues and flourishes thanks precisely to this continuation of individual contributions.

Famous names, on the other hand, come and go. Without the support of people to pass on your tradition, it dies with you. With the support of followers, a tradition of any longevity evolves and embraces new thinking, becoming more, or different from the vision of its founder. There would seem to be a conflict between the desires of a lone person who wishes to be famous for something, and the nature of a tradition. I think to be a true future ancestor of tradition, is to be part of that tradition and working within it, not trying to co-opt it for personal gain or fix it eternally in your own image.

Self as ancestor

Whether we intend it or not, we will be ancestors of one type or another. We have no control over what happens to our stories after we have gone, and no guarantee anything of ours will survive us in a meaningful way. We cannot control what the future will do with us, but we can try to shape it. If we leave nothing behind, there will be nothing for anyone else to find or respond to.

Thinking about the future that lies beyond our lifespan is not unlike thinking about the possibility of judgment after death. We can't really know what the criteria will be for assessing us, or even if there are any. What matters most is how we live now. Contemplating the possibility of afterlife judgment, karmic implications, the opinion of posterity or any other measuring stick you find resonant, is mostly useful in terms of what it tells us about the present.

Have I done anything that might be worthy of remembering? If I died tomorrow, what would I leave, both the good and the bad? Am I living my life in a way that makes me a good ancestor of the future? Am I living in a way that my own ancestors would think well of?

We measure ourselves against our own expectations, beliefs and fears. It is not an easy thing to do honestly, abandoning ego-assumptions that *of course* we are doing something significant or abdication assumptions that *of course* we don't matter at all. Perhaps the greater part of our legacy will be the harm we have caused, not the good we did in this life. It's not difficult to play up the importance of the things we value, and to play down the negative impact of behavior we don't really want to take responsibility for. The future will not judge us on what we wanted to do, or on what we would have done if only it had been made easy for us. The future, if it remembers us at all, will do so based on the things we did, and the things we did not do. All of our excuses will very likely die with us.

Ancestors of future Druidry

One of the biggest issues I think modern Druidry faces, is how to position itself with regards to the past. Current thinking makes it difficult if not impossible to claim any truly ancient lineage for Druidry, whilst at the same time there is undoubtedly a vital and longstanding ancestry of inspiration.

Phillip Carr-Gomm sums it up thus: 'After two centuries of ambivalent history, Druidism has finally emerged over the last forty years to offer a spiritual way that genuinely draws on ancient heritage for inspiration while making no claim to be identical to the Druidism that was practiced two thousand years ago.'[54]

Any new archaeological find has the potential to shift the official stories about Celts and Druids alike. All it takes is one grave with a golden sickle in it, and we'll have to throw out what we thought we didn't know, and start over. One blackened pit that turns out to be charred willow with a mix of animal and human remains would be all you would need to revitalize the image of Druids burning their victims in wicker men. One discovery of a missing, or previously unknown classical text could put all the writing we have in a different context, validating or dismissing or further obfuscating any or all of it. Equally, as further studies occur in the field of Welsh literature and those other writings that might or might not be mediaeval, we may yet find new twists in the story.

How we position ourselves now requires the flexibility to handle new information as it comes in. To me, it seems that the only viable position to take is therefore one of uncertainty. We don't know how things were. We can from there go on to speculate, so long as we remain clear about that. I am very taken with Graeme Talboys' thinking around the issue of where Druids are, and are not visible in Roman writing. If the Druids were the intellectual class, then lack of specific mention of them is simply because 'Druid' is an overview term, an imposition from outside of limited usefulness, and that most of the time it makes more sense to talk about 'Druids' in regard to the particular function they were carrying out. It also as a theory speaks to the means of survival – this is not a purely religious class, readily wiped out, it is the entire intellectual class of the Celts, so of course it survived to some degree. Once you consider that Celtic culture might not have separated religious and non-religious functions in the way we do, there is plenty of room for this story. I like it, it serves us well and contains plenty of room to flex if available knowledge changes.

We pick a story that says yes, Druids existed, and yes, we know enough about them to be inspired by that, and yes there is meaning in what we do. The story we choose places us in the wider consensus reality and informs our chances of being taken seriously. It also informs how we perceive ourselves. The reconstructionist ancestors, with their ever more elaborate, involved and self important histories had varying degrees of success when it came to being taken seriously. Looking back at their posturing and costumes, I have to wonder what any of them thought they were doing. That too is part of the story of how we got to here. For all their eccentricity and ego mania, they too left us a great deal of inspirational material to work with along with some very important lessons about how not to do things.

We can step away from issues around the literal truth of the past and work with our stories as stories. The path of inspiration is a far less confusing one. We can stride out on our own terms, offering new ideas as new, and letting them stand on their own merit. In this regard, I have been greatly inspired by Kevan Manwaring's The Way of Awen[55]. It is a book about now, about our own stories and our own creative responses to older stories. There is nothing to stop any of us from creating entirely new and original stories about how we want the world to be, and who we wish to be within it. Whether we want to call that vision 'Druid' or not, I don't know, but it's a good word, and the mystery and uncertainty inherent in it should stop any of us from getting too comfortably dogmatic, and that has to be a good thing.

A Personal Conclusion

Coming to the end of this book, I feel more keenly that I am at the beginning of a personal journey than I did when I started. I had imagined the writing process as a way of crystallizing my own thoughts. In some regards it has. I'm a lot clearer on my own feelings about human remains in museums than I was when I started. I've also worked through a lot of ideas about my own ancestry. There have been thought forms that only came together for me as I was in the process of trying to write something else entirely. It is not the book I imagined I was going to write, but in truth they seldom are.

One of the things I feel obliged to tackle in a more personal way is the idea of future ancestors of tradition. I've spent previous chapters talking about leaders, and placing myself as a small contributor mostly concerned with passing things along rather than leaving a name that will be remembered. Conscious that I am writing a book, I realize this may sound disingenuous. From a practical perspective, I've read far more books than I have written, and it has been more useful to think as a reader, than as an author some of the time.

I think without the belief that what you write, or do will have an impact, it would be difficult to muster sufficient motivation for the long hours of research, thought and creative effort required for any big project. I also think that everything and anything we do has the potential to achieve impact in unexpected ways, and that going into everything with that same sense of purposefulness is important. Normal, sensible attitudes to life strip from us all sense that what we do is significant. I think we are all encouraged, in both overt and subtle ways, to discount ourselves. We are small. We will be forgotten. There is no point grasping after dreams because you won't get there. This is the voice of 'sense' as many understand it, and it is not the voice that directs me.

Dreaming is one of the most important things we can do. Dreaming is the beginning of all new things, all creativity, innovation, all hope lies in what we can dream.

What am I dreaming, in writing this book? I'm dreaming for myself that writing books could be a viable way to earn a living. I am also dreaming of other ways of seeing the world, other stories that change how we perceive ourselves. I am dreaming that it is possible to be happy without needing to be buried alive under material possessions. More than anything, I am dreaming that the ideas I've waved about here might be resonant enough, strong enough to travel off without me and become part of something bigger.

If none of our ancestors had dared to dream, where would we be now?

Endnotes

1   Ellen Evert Hopman, *Scottish Herbs and Fairy Lore*, Pendraig Publishing, 2010, page 14 in the pdf version.

2   Philip Carr-Gomm, *What do Druids Believe?* Granta Books, 2006, page 9

3   Stuart Piggott, *The Druids*, Book Club Associates, 1977, page 15

4   Mark Lindsey Earley, *The Bardic Chair and Bardic Gorsedd of Caer Wyse*, 2012

5   Peter Berresford Ellis, *The Fabrication of 'Celtic' Astrology* , The Astrological Journal (vol 39. n. 4, 1997),

6   Peter Berresford Ellis, *The Fabrication of 'Celtic' Astrology* , The Astrological Journal (vol 39. n. 4, 1997),

7   Ronald Hutton, *The Pagan Religions of the Ancient British Isles*, Blackwell 1991 page 320

8   Clarissa Pinkola Estes, *Women Who Run with the Wolves*, Rider May, 1998

9   Edward Vallance, *A Radical History of Britain*, Abacus, 2009

10 Philip Carr-Gomm, *What do Druids Believe?* Granta Books, 2006 page 1

11 W.K. Wimsatt and Monroe Beardsley, *The Intentional Fallacy*, 1946

12 Stevie Davies, *Unbridled Spirits, Women of the English Revolution 1640-1660*, The Women's Press, 1998, page 2

13 Edward Vallance, *A Radical History of Britain*, Abacus, 2009, page 47

14 Stuart Piggott, *The Druids*, Book Club Associates 1977, page 10

15 Stuart Piggott, *The Druids*, Book Club Associates 1977, page 93

16 Simon James and Valery Rigby, *Britain and the Celtic Iron Age*, British Museum Press 1997, page 3

17 Edward Vallance, *A Radical History of Britain*, Abacus 2009 page 128

18 Stevie Davies, *Unbridled Spirits, Women of the English Revolution 1640-1660*, The Women's Press LTD 1998 page 7

19 Herbert Butterfield ,*The Whig Interpretation of History*, Norton 1965 p11

20 http://www.bbc.co.uk/blogs/thereporters/markeaston/2 011/02/happiness_work_sleep_and_bicyc.html

21 Stevie Davies, *Unbridled Spirits*, Women of the English Revolution 1640-1660, The Women's Press LTD 1998 page 189

22 Herbert Butterfield ,*The Whig Interpretation of History*, Norton 1965 p9

23 Stuart Piggott, *The Druids*, Book Club Associates, 1977, page 16

24 Ernest Jones, *The song of the lower classes.*

25 Edward Vallance, *A Radical History of Britain*, Abacus, 2009, page 14

26 by L. P. Hartley, *The Go Between*, 1953

27 Ronald Hutton, *The Pagan Religions of the Ancient British Isles*, Blackwell, 1991, page 133

28 Stuart Piggott, *The Druids*, Book Club Associates, 1977, pages 21, 95 and 97

29 Herbert Butterfield, *The Whig Interpretation of History*, Norton 1965 page 2

30 Graeme K Talboys, *The Druid Way*, page 48

31 Norma Jackson, *Druid Grave Found*, http://www.wvwnews .net/story.php?id=3415

32 Stephen Wilson, *The Magical Universe*, Hambledon and London, 2000, page xxx

33 Ronald Hutton, *The Pagan Religions of the Ancient British Isles*, Blackwell, 1991, page 118

34 Ronald Hutton, *The Pagan Religions of the Ancient British Isles*, Blackwell, 1991, page 144

35 Anne Ross and Don Robins, *The Life and Death of a Druid Prince*, Simon & Schuster, 1991

36 Stevie Davies, *Unbridled Spirits, Women of the English Revolution 1640-1660*, The Women's Press, 1998, page 6

37 N.M and R. Dauenhaur, *Stars Above, Earth Below* edited by Marsha C. Bol, Published by Robert Rinehart Publishers, 1998, page 3

38 Robin Herne, *Old Gods, New Druids*, O-Books, 2009, Page 61

39 Robin Herne, *Old Gods, New Druids*, O-Books, 2009, Page 66

40 Oliver Rackham, *The History of the Countryside: The Classic History of Britain's Landscape, Flora and Fauna*, Phoenix Press, 2001

41 Kevan Manwaring, *Turning the Wheel*, O-Books, 2011, page 216

42 Gregory Schrempp, *Stars Above, Earth Below* edited by Marsha C. Bol, Published by Robert Rinehart Publishers, 1998, page 20

43 Edward Vallance, *A Radical History of Britain*, Abacus, 2009, page 5

44 Simon James and Valery Rigby, *Britain and the Celtic Iron Age*, British Museum Press 1997, page 61

45 Graeme K Talboys, *The Druid Way*, page 7

46 Stephen Wilson, *The Magical Universe*, Hambledon and London, 2000

47 Kevan Manwaring, *Turning the Wheel*, O-Books, 2011, page 42

48 Published by O-Books 2012

49 The Capuchin Crypt beneath the Capuchin Church of the Immaculate Conception (1645)

50 http://mg.co.za/article/2011-10-05-returned-namibian-skulls-ignite-anger-not-peace/ (Mail and Guardian online, October 2011)

51 http://www.bbc.co.uk/news/science-environment-15822232

52 Anne B Ryan, *Enough is Plenty*, O-Books,

53 Ronald Hutton, *Blood and Mistletoe*, Yale University Press,

2009, page 182

54 Philip Carr-Gomm, *What do Druids Believe?* Granta Books, 2006, p24

55 Kevan Manwaring, *The Way of Awen*, O-Books, 2010

Moon Books invites you to begin or deepen your encounter with Paganism, in all its rich, creative, flourishing forms.

Printed and bound by CPI Group (UK) Ltd, Croydon, CR0 4YY